RENAISSANCE FLORENCE
ON FIVE FLORINS A DAY

*Florence is today one of
Europe's most civilized,
cultured and artistically rich
cities – thanks in large part to
its immensely powerful banks.*

Charles FitzRoy

RENAISSANCE FLORENCE
ON FIVE FLORINS
A DAY

with 86 illustrations, 16 in colour

 Thames & Hudson

CONTENTS

I · PREPARATION
AND ARRIVAL

The year 1490, when the most beautiful city renowned for abundance, victories, arts and noble buildings profoundly enjoyed health and peace.

INSCRIPTION IN GHIRLANDAIO'S FRESCO
OF THE ANGEL APPEARING TO
ZACHARIAS, SANTA MARIA NOVELLA

There are so many reasons to visit Tuscany in the year of Our Lord 1490. If you are a merchant, you may be heading for the textile markets of Florence and Lucca. If you are a parent, perhaps you intend to send your children to study under one of the great humanist teachers in Florence or Arezzo, or at the universities of Pisa or Siena. If you are a pilgrim, you may be following the via Francigena through San Gimignano and Siena on your way to Rome, or off to visit the pilgrimage churches, where miraculous images of the Virgin appeared only recently in Prato and Cortona. If you are visiting just for enjoyment, there are numerous exciting festivals to watch. Some are religious, such as the Feast of Saint John the Baptist in Florence; others are secular, notably the Palio in Siena and the Giostra del Saracino in Arezzo. You may want to see all the wonderful works of art that are becoming the talk of Europe: the great dome of the Cathedral in

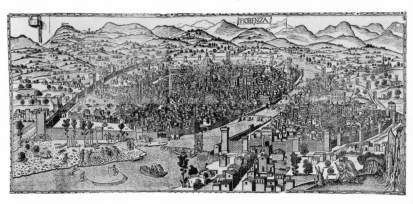

This detailed view of Florence allows you to identify the major churches and palaces within the walls. Four bridges span the Arno flowing through the centre of the city; on the banks fishermen haul in their catch. Note the artist sketching the view in the foreground.

There is no mistaking the flattened nose and severe frown of Lorenzo de' Medici, the effective ruler of Florence. This bust is by Andrea del Verrocchio.

Florence, the paintings of Leonardo da Vinci, and the sculpture of Donatello.

Wherever you go in Tuscany, the food and drink are excellent (some of the best wine in Italy comes from the area), the countryside is beautiful, adorned with the villas of the rich, and every church is filled with precious relics and works of art. The shops are packed with tempting goods, and there is never a dull moment watching vociferous Tuscans gossiping, arguing, doing deals and flirting in the street.

Before you arrive, it is as well to know a little Tuscan history, it will stand you in good stead. Most of Tuscany is dominated by the Florentine Republic and, wherever you go, you will see the Medici *palle* (balls) prominently displayed (Lorenzo de' Medici is the *de facto* ruler of Florence). But Florence has taken control of the major cities only relatively recently so be aware that some locals, such as the Pisans, feel aggrieved that they are compelled to pay lip-service to Florence. There are also two bastions of independence: Siena and Lucca, the latter of which is incredibly rich despite its diminutive size. In Siena you will be immediately aware of the deep and abiding hostility to Florence, whom the Sienese perceive as a bullying neighbour, so try to keep the F word out of your conversation.

A BRIEF DESCRIPTION
OF FLORENCE

Florence is full of all imaginable wealth,
She defeats her enemies in war and in
*   civil strife,*
She enjoys the favour of fortune and has
*   a powerful population,*
Successfully she fortifies and conquers
*   castles,*
She reigns over the sea and the land and
*   the whole of the world,*
Under her leadership the whole of
*   Tuscany enjoys happiness.*
Like Rome she is always triumphant.

INSCRIPTION ON THE FAÇADE OF
THE PALAZZO DELLA PODESTÀ

Florence is far and away the most important city in Tuscany, and you are likely to spend a great deal of time there during your visit. The city stands right in the centre of the province, dominating the valley of the Arno, 50 miles inland from the sea. Even the air is favourable (or at least that is what the locals claim), halfway between the rarified atmosphere of Arezzo and the heavy air of Pisa. Florence has a population of about 75,000 and ranks alongside Venice, Milan, Naples, Paris and Salamanca as one of the greatest cities in Europe, certainly larger than London or Rome.

The river Arno runs through the city, a mere stream in the hottest months, but prone to violent flooding in the winter. The city centre, with all the main civil and religious buildings, stands on the north bank, and encompasses the area between the Piazza della Signoria, the centre of government, and the Piazza del Duomo, where the Cathedral and Bap-

Here we see the two most important buildings in Florence: on the right, the forbidding Palazzo della Signoria, with its unmistakable campanile; and in the background, Brunelleschi's great dome rising above the Cathedral.

tistery stand. This is a relatively small but extremely interesting area, which takes just twenty minutes to cross by foot. But there is much of interest to see on the Oltrarno, as the south bank is known. The majority of the fifty squares in the city serve as backdrops to the main churches.

The main markets in the city are the Mercato Vecchio (Old Market), the site of the old Roman Forum and the main food market, and the Mercato Nuovo (New Market), where bankers and money-lenders ply their trade. If you ever need to call on their services, you will need a basic knowledge of the florin, the common currency throughout Tuscany. A florin is worth seven lire, and a lira is worth twenty soldi or sixty quattrini.

THE TUSCAN DIALECT

That thankless, malignant people, who of old came down from Fiesole, and still smack of the mountain and the rock.

DANTE ON HIS FELLOW FLORENTINES, IN *INFERNO*

You will also need to have some understanding of the Tuscan dialect, which everybody speaks and writes here and which they use in commerce as well. This practice goes back to the last century, when the three greatest writers in Italy – Dante, Boccaccio and Petrarch – all routinely used the language in their works. At the same time Dominican and Franciscan friars, whom you will come across in every

town you visit, use the vernacular in their preaching and writing – they know the best way to hold the concentration of their audiences. Lorenzo de' Medici is a great champion of the Tuscan dialect, and uses it for all his writings, both in prose and poetry. He considers it the perfect way to express his thoughts and emotions, and argues that, unlike Latin, which is a dead language and a linguistic straitjacket, Tuscan has the ability to change, adapt and develop.

As Lorenzo is the most powerful man in Tuscany, many people have followed his lead, though pompous lawyers still love to use Latin, no doubt reckoning that, with their superior wisdom, their *a priori*s and *pro bono*s (how typical of a lawyer to offer something for free in Latin so nobody will understand him) will confuse their clients, so that they can double their charges. Lorenzo, however (as you will find out) never does anything without having an ulterior motive. He knows that the spread of the Tuscan language will enhance Florence's reputation abroad, and he is also aware that, with the advent of the exciting new science of printing, more and more people are reading books and this will speed up the process.

If you want to gain a further insight into Tuscan literature, you can read some key books before you set out, notably Dante's *Divine Comedy*, which is full of insights into his fellow Tuscans; but be warned, it is a mammoth work. You can get a quicker insight into the Florentine mind by reading Boccaccio's *Decameron*, written in the aftermath of the Black Death, or Petrarch's love poetry. If you are looking for facts, Giovanni Villani's *Florentine Chronicle*, all eight volumes of it, is stuffed full of them. If you want to gain an understanding of humanism, which is all the rage among well-educated Florentines, read the books of Leon Battista Alberti. If you are interested in art, his books on painting and architecture (the latter published recently in ten volumes), have been extremely influential, as has his treatise *The Family*, which gives an excellent idea of how the Florentines you meet approach the subjects of education, marriage, household management and money.

ARRIVAL

There are a number of ways to reach Tuscany but you are well advised to travel in company. All sorts of thieves and undesirables frequent the roads. Keep your purse under your bolster at night, make sure your horse or mule is well looked after, and keep your eyes open. Many a traveller has arrived at his destination with far fewer of his worldly goods than when he set out.

If you are coming from the north, two major routes from Milan and Venice converge on Bologna from where you must cross the mountains, known as the Apennines, to reach Florence. Further east a good road runs parallel to the mountains passing through Arezzo and on to Perugia. If you are coming from the south the route is much easier, particularly if you head up the old Roman via Aurelia to Pisa, or the via Cassia, which goes to Siena and on to Florence.

If you are coming by boat (normally safer and less arduous, providing you survive the tempests and the Turkish ships that terrorize the eastern Mediterranean) you can land at Pisa. Then you continue up the Arno valley to Florence. The river is navigable almost to the gates of the city, and you can enjoy a leisurely journey upstream, pulled by oxen plodding up the riverbank. However, the river is shallow and sluggish in summer, with artificial barriers and sand deposits, and prone to floods during spring and autumn. Most travellers prefer the parallel route by land, which takes in the cities of Lucca, Pistoia and Prato. An alternative route into Tuscany is on the via Francigena, much favoured by pilgrims travelling from France to Rome. It passes through Lucca, San Gimignano and Siena, all of which have profited greatly from the pilgrims' passing trade – it was once the most popular pilgrimage route in Europe after those to Santiago de Compostela and Jerusalem.

II · FLORENTINES AT HOME

I always keep my papers ... locked up in my study, into which I never allow my wife to enter.

ALBERTI

As you walk through the streets on your way to your lodgings – perhaps the Snail tavern near the Old Market, which has a good reputation – you may well wonder what sort of life Florentines enjoy behind the façades of those stern palaces, with their rusticated stonework and small, barred windows deliberately placed above eye level. Despite their uninviting appearance, there are always a group of people seated on benches outside the most important ones, waiting for an interview. The best way to gain admittance is to do business with the owner. If you want to buy some clothes, for example, you will be taken in to see the showroom on the ground floor of a cloth merchant's palazzo, filled with bolts of cloth in an array of tempting colours, with camphor and salts in pomades suspended from the ceiling to keep away the moths.

If you are a keen purchaser and become a favoured client, you may be invited upstairs to the owner's study, known as a *studiolo* or *scrittoio* (writing room), where he stores his business and personal records. It tends to be cluttered with desks, tables to count money, coin caskets, chests, shelves and cupboards for documents, accounting books, loose papers, bundles of letters, weighing scales and perhaps some maps. If you make a good impression, you may also be permitted to see his private treasures, including jewels and collections of antique coins and medals. Some owners like to work in comfort; Francesco Sassetti, the Medici banker, has a connecting room heated by a fireplace and containing a bath. To judge from his disastrous results as manager, perhaps he spends too much time in the latter.

You may also receive a social invitation to visit a palace, in which case you will see the grandest rooms in the house, situated on the *piano nobile*.

Only the wealthiest merchants can afford a pair of spectacles – invaluable for poring over their ledgers.

One of Luca della Robbia's enamelled terracottas of the Labours of the Months set into the ceiling of Lorenzo's study in Palazzo Medici.

ourful frescoes and murals painted on the walls. Panelled rooms have paintings set into the wainscoting and sometimes a *tondo* (a circular religious painting that is often found in Florence) on the wall. Tapestries from Flanders provide additional colour, while ceramics from the Montelupo factory situated just outside the city are also very popular. Some palaces now have glass in the windows though most still rely on shutters to keep out the cold (though not the draft).

Towards the rear, on the quieter side of the house, are a series of bedrooms for members of the household, some with a bathtub in an adjoining chamber. The master bedroom contains an elaborately carved bed, often the most expensive object in the house. It is a status symbol, since so much social activity is based around it: birth, sickness and death, all of which take place semi-publicly. Underneath the bed is a discreet scattering of mulberry twigs, designed to attract the fleas that tend to infest the mattresses and bolsters. Other items of furniture include a daybed, chests or *cassoni*, a mirror and a devotional work, either painted or carved. In the corner stands a basin for washing. In the winter a brazier or bed warmer will be brought into the bedroom. Many palaces have a loggia on the top floor where members of the household can take the fresh air. It can be used as an open-air dining room, though it also makes the best place to dry the washing.

A large, spacious hall, known as the *salone*, with a long table, is used for formal occasions, banquets, receptions and family gatherings. It faces onto the street, and it is from the *salone*'s windows that women watch processions during Carnival. In the centre of the room stands the fireplace, around which the family congregates during winter.

A dining room and a number of smaller chambers and antechambers are located off this central room. They are often richly decorated with multicoloured brocades, velvets and damasks. Bright, geometrically patterned carpets are draped carefully over tables, chairs and window seats, much too precious to be placed on the floor. They complement the col-

As far as possible, latrines are placed out of the way, in a cupboard beneath a staircase. Everyone knows that the Black Death was caused by poisonous odours in the air, so every effort is made to prevent noxious vapours affecting the humours of the rest of the household. Various methods are used: bags filled with violet or rose blooms in chests or beneath mattresses, pomanders and perfume-burners giving off the scent of amber or musk. Ladies who can afford it are encouraged to wear perfumed gloves, necklaces and pendants. But the most enticing smells come from the kitchen, a mixture of roasting meat, smoky fire, cloves, saffron, crushed basil and garlic.

The mistress of the house does her best to make the interior as comfortable as possible. She knows she will spend a very large proportion of her life at home. There is, however, little time to relax. She has much to supervise: inspecting the linen washed in a solution of ashes and perfumed with quince apples, making sure the well drainer has turned up, checking that the maids are mending all the old clothes and that the kitchen fire is safe. In every room servants are hard at work, sweeping floors with brooms, scrubbing pots or filling warming pans with coal. When she has a free moment, the mistress can venture outside into the garden to admire the herbs she has planted: sage, rosemary, stonewart and basil.

There is a large gap between the lives of the rich and the poor. Artisans and workers can only dream of the life-style of the patricians in their splendid palaces. They dwell in less exalted neighbourhoods, in small, insubstantial wooden houses of two or three storeys, one room per storey, no more than 15 feet wide, with one family per floor. Many labourers aspire to nothing more than having their own entrance to the building they live in, or, if they are even luckier, a separate staircase. Some families have to make do with a single-room cottage. Life in these small houses centres on the kitchen, which serves as a family room for eating and playing games. In winter this is the warmest room in the house, with the family huddled round the fire.

COURTSHIP

If you happen to come across the splendid sight of a bride on a white horse being led through the streets, you may well want to learn about the ritual surrounding the wedding. It is a subject that Florentines take very seriously and that gives an insight into their character. As you might expect from a nation of astute businessmen, there is a great deal of negotiation involved between the two families, particularly in matches between the richer Florentine dynasties. These are often arranged marriages, with a wide discrepancy in age between the groom in his early thirties and the bride still in her teens.

The most complex negotiations concern the dowry (see below). Once the two families have completed these negotiations, a little romance is allowed into the proceedings. The agreement is celebrated at the bride's house with the happy couple stating their wish to marry and making vows before a notary, with males of both families acting as witnesses. The couple clasp hands and exchange rings, a highly symbolic moment, as Florentines believe that rings have very special qualities. The notary then declares the couple betrothed and to make sure this is legal, the contract is signed in the study.

There is often a gap of several months between the betrothal and the marriage itself. During this period it is perfectly acceptable for the couple to show their affection for one another, and few parents object even when the young lovers sleep together. Sometimes, however, the husband-to-be goes too far in his advances, taking advantage of his betrothed's innocence. Braccio Martelli boasted to Lorenzo how his friend Niccolo Ardinghelli, whose manhood he compared with a 'bull's horn', deflowered his fiancée while Martelli stood guard.

Normally, however, all is peace and harmony, and the bride's family uses the time to arrange a trousseau, consisting of a number of ornate gowns, with richly embroidered and detach-

able sleeves, other items of clothing, jewelry, linen and a collection of personal items: hairbrushes, combs, a mirror, sewing paraphernalia and some devotional books. Meanwhile, the groom's family are busy organizing the splendid feast that will follow the marriage.

THE WEDDING

With the assistance of a ladder, the groom, flanked by witnesses, reached the bride, and facing each other they pronounced the formula of the ritual, balanced in an equilibrium as unstable as the tie that thus bound them.

AN EYEWITNESS RECORDS A WEDDING ON A FLORENTINE BALCONY

On the auspicious day of the wedding the two families celebrate the happy event in church after which the husband brings his bride to his home on a white horse, heading a procession through the streets with attendants, musicians and dancers. Ever conscious of their social status, and the importance of the match, the bride's family include a lavish display of silver and gilt tableware in the procession and the trousseau is put on public show (to make sure the husband is getting his dues two independent dealers provide a valuation).

The husband gives his bride her wedding clothes, often with his emblem to show that she is now part of his family. When Marco Parenti married Caterina Strozzi, from one of the grandest Florentine families, he gave her a gown of crimson velvet and a silk surcoat, a pearl-studded hat, and a crimson silk belt (a well-known symbol of fertility) 'because she's so beautiful and he wants her to look even more so', as Caterina's mother Alessandra noted approvingly. In typical Florentine fashion, the shrewd mother also calculated that her daughter's clothes were worth 400 florins, and wondered whether Caterina's hat with its 800 peacock feathers adorned with pearls and enamelled flowers was really worth it. The government, anxious to curtail this conspicuous consumption, has issued an edict declaring that the bride cannot wear gold or silver jewelry, pearls, crimson cloth or furs, but this is universally ignored.

Once the procession has arrived at the bride's house, there is a great feast with a tiered buffet laden with tempting dishes: spiced veal, roast kid, fish pie flavoured with oranges, roasted peacocks' tongues, a pie stuffed with live blackbirds, salads, sweetmeats, nutmeg, saffron, sugared almonds and candied fruits. Sometimes a literary figure will sing a song, or declaim a piece of prose or verse specially composed for the occasion, though he has to compete with jugglers and musicians. The revelry continues until

We stood talking a while, and then the bride and groom were put to bed, and we all went up with them right to the bed, laughing at them.

A LETTER TO A BRIDE'S FATHER

the couple retire to bed. If they are deemed to be ill-matched the more inebriated guests proceed to shout rude insults at their bedroom window.

The next morning, to celebrate the union, the bride is given a hearty breakfast consisting of eggs representing fertility and sweetmeats for love. It is now the groom's turn to give the bride a counter-trousseau, a symbolic gesture showing her integration into his family. It often contains some fine clothing, pieces of jewelry and a marriage chest or strong box, known as a *cassone* or *forziere*,

THE SYMBOLISM OF RINGS

There is a great deal of symbolism attached to rings.
Rubies, as you might guess from their fiery red colour, symbolize a heart burning with love; they also promote health and dispel bad thoughts.
Diamonds ensure conjugal fidelity, maintain harmony between man and wife, and provide antidotes to all ills.
Emeralds repel disease and assist women in childbirth, as well as increasing wealth and strengthening eyesight.
Sapphires and pearls are for those who want a quiet life: they encourage peace, piety and chastity.

THE DOWRY

This costs a small fortune, as much as 1,400 florins, and sometimes even 2,000 for a really good match. When Lorenzo de' Medici married his aristocratic wife she brought a dowry of 6,000 florins with her from Rome. Considering that even the best-paid lawyer is unlikely to earn more than 500 florins per annum, it is no wonder that so many eligible young women end up as nuns (though not all enter wholeheartedly into this vocation and there have been a number of scandals – see Chapter VII).

There are all sorts of stipulations attached to the contract. If the dowry is unpaid, the husband is allowed to send his wife back to her family, a humiliating fate. The Medici insisted that Lorenzo could return his wife if she did not bear children.

There have been a number of bitter disputes when the family of a husband who dies insists that his widow repays her dowry should she get remarried.

Most rich Florentines, like good businessmen, start paying money into the Dowry Bank (*Monte dei Doti*), a communal fund set up to guarantee a dowry on their daughter's marriage. It is treated as a taxable asset.

The government uses the money over a fifteen-year period, after which the girl is deemed eligible for marriage.

Some people reckon the amount in the Dowry Bank accounts for half the assets in the city.

A Florentine wedding is great cause for celebration. Here elegantly dressed couples dance beneath a striped canopy.

decorated with paintings showing scenes of marital prudence and self-lessness, taken from classical or chivalric tales. This seems a wonderfully romantic gesture but there is a catch. It is only a loan and the objects are normally reclaimed and very often pawned or sold after a few years.

Lower-class Florentines, of course, cannot afford any of these elaborate gestures. They have little interest in wealth and breeding, preferring good health, physical strength and a willingness to work, all of which are more important than a decent dowry. They indulge in none of the ritual that their grand fellow citizens love so much. Prospective couples meet in church, during religious processions, during harvest, at market or at evening gatherings where the young dance together. To show his devotion, the young man gives his girl ribbons, handkerchiefs, rings or coins, and in return, if he is fortunate, he will receive a lock of her hair. When the couple have become betrothed, few artisans bother with bans or vows. Indeed, you may come across tales of Florentines who have tied the knot in highly unlikely places: a tavern, a kitchen, a stable, or outside in a garden or beside a fountain.

CHILDBIRTH AND CHILDHOOD

Tell your wife that she has done much better than my wife, who made eight girls before she made my son.

FEDERICO DA MONTEFELTRO TO
LORENZO DE' MEDICI, 1472

With the acute dangers that women face in childbirth, Florentines take every precaution. The pregnant woman reads the legend of St Margaret, patron saint of childbirth, and how she emerged unharmed from the belly of a dragon. If the family is illiterate, the book is placed on the stomach of the woman in labour. Coral is regarded as an effective talisman, warding off evil and preventing excessive bleeding. To help with a safe delivery, women take mandrake root or coriander seeds, or, if they have strong stomachs, various concoctions containing pulverized snakeskins, rabbit milk and crayfish. The more

I cannot tell you, Magnificent Father, how glad I am to have the pony, and how his arrival incites me to work... He is so handsome and so perfect that the trumpet of Maronius would hardly suffice to sing his praises. You may think how I love him; particularly when his joyous neighs resound and rejoice the neighbourhood.

THE SEVEN-YEAR-OLD PIERO DE'
MEDICI TO HIS FATHER LORENZO

religious have threads that touched the Virgin's Girdle in Prato. To show how dangerous childbirth is, the pragmatic Alessandra Strozzi took out insurance for 12 florins for her daughter Caterina on the birth of her first child; others take a more cavalier approach, betting on the sex of the child.

After birth the mother is given a special diet of poultry with a generous dose of salt. Often she is presented with a birthtray, perhaps with a representation of a young boy or a putto, as every Florentine man dreams of producing a son and heir. Lorenzo de' Medici still has the one given to his mother on his birth hanging on his bedroom wall. In many churches you will see silver or wax ex-votos, with images of swaddled babies, donated by grateful parents.

The baby is baptized within a few days of birth, or sometimes, if the infant is in danger, within a few hours.

A birthtray depicts two youths playing a game of civettino. *Note how one contestant stands on the foot of the other.*

whole tender age is more properly assigned to women's quiet care than to the active attention of men.'

Florentines are naturally fond of children, and you will find that younger girls and boys are indulged with 'little wooden horses, pretty cymbals, counterfeit birds, gilded drums' and that their parents make a great fuss of them, 'holding them in [their] arms, kissing them, singing them songs,' in the words of Fra Giovanni Dominici, who wrote a handbook on child education.

You will often see proud fathers heading for the Baptistery where they make a record of the birth in the civic register with a bean, black for a boy and white for a girl. At the christening the child's sponsors present gifts: special bread, marzipan cakes, boxes of sweetmeats and candles. The more generous ones place coins in the baby's swaddling, or give a piece of silver in a special holder, or a figurine depicting Hercules or St John the Baptist, symbol of the city.

Immediately after the baptism, the baby is handed over to a wet nurse, usually a peasant woman out in the country. For the first year of his life, the infant remains in swaddling clothes. He or she is then dressed in a tunic or skirt. This is a world dominated by women, as Alberti instructed earlier this century: 'It seems to me that this

FUNERALS

Like weddings, death is another way for a Florentine family to proclaim its position in society. You will know one has occurred when you see black woollen cloth hung from the windows of a palace. Soon temporary benches will be installed in the streets en route to the chosen church to provide physical comfort for the mourners. When a public official or a doctor of law or medicine dies or 'enters the great sea' (as Florentines refer to death) his funeral is accompanied by banners bearing his coat-of-arms and emblems of his profession. Families often choose to dress the corpse in the habit of the confraternity or religious order of which he was a member. Brown is the traditional colour of mourning, though it hardly seems necessary for the Commune, interfering as ever, to proclaim that women's dresses must be properly buttoned up so that their breasts are fully covered.

The pageantry surrounding grander funerals is a relatively recent development and some older Florentines complain of the change in standards. They think that a low-key funeral shows more respect to the departed and look back to the old custom when a body was dressed in white muslin lined with taffeta, placed on a plain paliasse, and buried without trappings of rank. Cosimo de' Medici may have been laid out in state in San Lorenzo when he died in 1464 so that the populace could pay their respects, but his tombstone was quite plain, with the simple but eloquent inscription *Pater Patriae*.

SLAVES

I must remind you that when Alfonso [her son] is weaned, we ought to get a little slave-girl to look after him, or else one of the black boys to keep him company.

A FLORENTINE LADY TO HER HUSBAND

For the love of God, in charity, so that she may find her child again.

A WRITTEN PLEA ACCOMPANYING A DONATION
FROM AN ANONYMOUS SLAVE WOMAN
TO THE FOUNDLING HOSPITAL

If you visit one of the grander palaces, you will find that, among the servants, there is invariably a female slave (the asking price in the market is about 50 florins). You will often see them running errands in the streets or shopping for their mistresses in the markets. Mostly they are Slavs or Tartars (regarded as hard-working), sometimes Russians, Greeks or even Africans. Some humanists object to the practice, but most people think it is perfectly acceptable – after all it is sanctioned in canon and civil law. Who can complain when the Pope himself has distributed among his cardinals one hundred negro slaves given to him by King Ferdinand of Aragon?

Most slaves are involved in domestic work. Their normal clothing is a coarse grey woollen habit with black cape, and there are regulations forbidding them from wearing 'coats or dresses or sleeves of any kind in any bright colours'. The majority are well looked after, and often are valued members of the household. When a prosperous notary freed his slave-girl Fresina, he gave her his best bed, lingerie and silver ornaments 'because if ever there was a loyal, honest and sober servant or slave, who loved her household and all the family warmly, it was her'. Bernardo Machiavelli engaged an eight-year-old girl for ten years, but when she 'said and did mad things and could not serve us', she was sent home to her parents, taking a new blouse and dress belonging to his daughters. Perhaps the slave girl was fed up with being bossed about. Her replacement was given reams of precise instructions: she was to sweep the dining room, wash up the plates, set the midday meal, help make bread and do the family washing.

Some slaves take liberties. The patrician Alessandra Strozzi wanted to punish her slave Caterinuccia but when the feisty slave threatened to spread gossip about Alessandra's daughter Lissandra, she backed down. Five years later, much to her annoyance, Caterinuccia was still a member of the household, paying scant attention to her mistress, 'for she stays in her own room, sometimes spinning a little for me, and sometimes attending to her own affairs.'

With a young, nubile girl living under the same roof, there is always the chance that she will attract the fancy of the master of the household. Numerous babies, delivered to the Foundling Hospital, are the products of these unions; there is a big advantage in pursuing this route since these babies are treated as neither illegitimate nor slaves. Both Lorenzo de' Medici's father and his grandfather had children by slaves and Cosimo's illegitimate son Carlo enjoyed a distinguished ecclesiastical career.

Not surprisingly, many wives are highly suspicious of their husbands. When the slave belonging to the respectable matron Monna Lucia, wife of a Florentine merchant, became pregnant, she was unable to discover who

> *He had no children from his wife Simona, although he did have several illegitimate offspring, some from a woman of good family, and some from a slave who was very beautiful, and whom he later married to someone from the Mugello.*
>
> GIOVANNI MORELLI ON HIS COUSIN

the father was and became consumed with jealousy. The merchant grumbled that his domestic life had become intolerable: 'she still will not believe me, whether I swear and coax…and now we have an old woman [her replacement] who is more like a monkey than a female; and this is the life I lead.' The government deems it acceptable for men to misbehave at home but imposes severe penalties for making another's slave pregnant: a fine of one third of the slave's value.

MEDICINE

For twenty days [he] had the warm waters poured through a pipe onto the crown of his head, for the physicians said this would be beneficial, since his brain was too moist.

POPE PIUS II TAKING THE BATHS AT PETRIOLO

The best advice if you are not feeling well is to try to sort out the problem yourself. If you must see a doctor, however, you will find the physician a major figure in Florentine society, with his long capacious robe trimmed with squirrel fur and bands of scarlet. There are some seventy doctors registered to practise in Florence, but there are many more who have no intention of registering. Lorenzo de' Medici, the most important man in Florence, has Moses the Jew acting as his personal doctor; he administers a mixture of bleeding, purging and poultices to try to lessen the pain of Lorenzo's gout, and is reputed to give his master pulverized pearls and diamonds to cure his stomach pains.

Many households have their own recipe books, which include cures for a multitude of ailments (they also contain advice on removing stains from fabrics and keeping at bay bedbugs, lice, fleas and spiders). There is much analysis of the four humours – choleric, stolid, melancholic and optimistic – that affect a person's actions and his health. It is widely accepted that there is a close relationship between the exterior and interior of the body. If a patient suffers from gallstones, for instance, he will have a concoction of honey and wool from a ram's testicles applied to his side. To keep his bowels regular his navel will be smeared with an ointment consisting of boiled sage mixed with pork fat.

One of the greatest fears of Florentines is the plague. They know that the traditional remedies – firing guns, ringing bells and playing mournful music – have been all too ineffectual. They are willing to try other remedies (applying aloes, myrrh and saffron), but none of these can be guaranteed to provide immunity. Better to flee the city and go deep into the countryside.

Florentines are also fascinated by medical advice on the question of sex, at least for men. Semen is regarded as a form of excrement, and must only be spent in moderation. There is no specific sexual advice for women; some things are too obvious to state, such as the wearing of a girdle that will make one irresistible. Instead, there is advice on how to deal with inflammation of the breasts, for inducing periods and for pregnancy. Bathing consists of a steam bath, a process of scrubbing and anointing to promote the expulsion of grime and sweat that could induce disease. Washing is therefore more than a mere physical process; for instance, washing one's hair in bran not only makes it beautiful, but also strengthens the brain and the memory. The most pleasurable and efficacious form of bathing is to go to a spa, of which there are quite a number throughout Tuscany; Lorenzo is a regular attendee.

In order to prevent the return of these pains, you must get a stone called sapphire, and have it set in gold, so that it should touch the skin. This must be worn on the third finger of the left hand. If this is done, the pains in the joints, or gouty pains, will cease, because the stone has occult virtues, and the specific one of preventing evil humours going to the joints.

A CURE FOR GOUT

III · OUT AND ABOUT WITH THE FLORENTINES

FINDING YOUR BEARINGS

You will now want to find your way round the city. It is divided into four quarters: in the centre, San Giovanni with the Cathedral and the Piazza della Signoria; to the north, Santa Maria Novella, stronghold of the Medici; to the east, Santa Croce; and to the south of the Arno, Santo Spirito, also known as the Oltrarno. These quarters, in turn, are subdivided into four 'gonfalons' (*gonfaloni*), each with its own emblem.

You will spend a great deal of time in the city centre, watching Florentines going about their business, admiring the main works of art and shopping in the markets. Everywhere you will see builders hard at work erecting handsome palaces – over thirty new ones have been built in the last fifty years and the towers that used to be such a feature of the skyline have largely been pulled down. The most important families dominate their neighbourhoods: the Medici on via Larga, in the area of San Lorenzo, the Strozzi around Santa Trinita.

The river Arno has played a crucial role in making Florence the economic powerhouse it is today, turning the mills and providing the water necessary for washing and dyeing wool. Four bridges cross the river. The Ponte Rubaconte, furthest upstream and built in 1237, is the oldest and longest, a sturdy structure consisting of six massive piles supporting houses, shops and a little chapel. Next comes the famous Ponte Vecchio (Old Bridge), erected in 1345, a noisy and busy thoroughfare covered in shops and houses. Downstream is the handsome Ponte Santa Trinita, dating from 1250, with a small hospice for monks and a stone sundial. Beyond stands the Ponte alla Carraia, constructed in 1304, after its predecessor collapsed under the weight of spectators gathered there to watch a representation of hell being performed on the river on May Day. It is named after the carts (*carri*) that carry the wool across the river between Ognissanti and the parish of San Frediano.

To facilitate the movement of government officials, traders and goods, a number of streets have been widened in the city centre. They have been paved with flagstones, with a footpath on each side and a gutter to carry rainwater down to the Arno, so that they are, at least theoretically, free of mud and slime. Many street names describe their trades: for example, Calzaiuoli

Above *View of the Arno with the Ponte Vecchio*. Above right *A view across the narrow thoroughfare of the Ponte Vecchio with the Cathedral beyond.*

(shoemakers), Tintori (dyers), Cimatori (shearers), Saponai (soapers) and Librai (booksellers). They form a contrast with the more run-down working-class neighbourhoods outside the city centre – for example, the area of Santa Croce to the east, where the dyeing and washing of the wool is carried out and where many artists have their workshops. Both here and in the Oltrarno, where cloth workers congregate in via Maggio, many houses have cloth hanging out to dry from wooden bars strung across the windows.

Some streets have nicknames, many of them insulting. If you live north of the river you tend to refer dismissively to borgo San Jacopo across the Arno as borgo Pidiglioso (Lousy Street). Northerners are even ruder about the area of Camaldoli, beyond the south-ern boundary of the city, maintaining that paupers are buried 'like beasts', refuse is dumped indiscriminately and homosexuals run rampant. You are advised to take them at their word and not investigate the area too closely, certainly not at night.

There is so much of interest to take in as you wander the streets. The most interesting of the city's thirty hospitals is the beautiful Foundling Hospital (Ospedale degli Innocenti) by Brunelleschi, next to the church of Santissima Annunziata, where you can see the wheel on which hundreds of foundling babies are placed when they are left for adoption. Many Florentines have spent years languishing in the austere, fortified Stinche, the state prison for bankrupts and debtors. Giovanni Villani wrote a fascinating history of his native city while incarcerated here.

Surrounding the city is a 40-foot-high fortified wall that extends for five miles, with forty-five towers each 75 feet high, catwalks and external

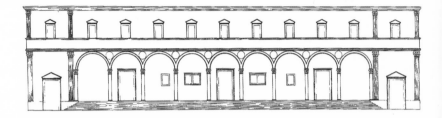

niches with sculpted saints. This wall is pierced by eleven well-guarded gates, which are locked at night, when the curfew is imposed. There are six on the north side of the Arno, five on the south side. The main ones are La Croce, San Gallo, al Prato and Faenza, and across the Arno, the Porta Romana. There are magnificent views back over the city from the gates across the river, the Porta San Pietro Gattolini, where many of the leading Florentines have villas, and the Porta San Giorgio, where jugglers congregate whenever there is a festival.

A DAY IN THE LIFE

What city, not merely in Italy, but in all the world, is more securely placed within its circle of walls, more proud in its palazzi, more bedecked with churches, more beautiful in its architecture, more imposing in its gates, richer in piazzas, happier in its wide streets, greater in its people, more glorious in its citizenry, more inexhaustible in wealth, more fertile in its fields?

COLUCCIO SALUTATI

The harmonious façade of Brunelleschi's Foundling Hospital, one of the city's foremost charitable institutions. It was the first building in the new classical style.

If you get up soon after dawn, or if perhaps you are on your way home after an exciting night's entertainment (of which Florence has plenty to offer), you will notice that Florentines are early risers. A few women are on their way to early mass, while apprentices hurry towards the *botteghe* where they work, tightening the belts on their tunics and trying to straighten their ill-fitting hose as they go. Servants make their way to their masters' houses, anxious to arrive before their mistress awakes. An occasional drunk, who has slept in a tavern to avoid breaking the curfew, staggers home. In the city centre, where most of the palaces have shops on the ground floor, workmen are busy opening the shutters and letting down hinged shelves on which they display their wares.

Further out, down by the Arno near the Franciscan church of Santa Croce, workers are laying out fleeces in preparation for washing. On the outskirts of the city members of the religious confraternities are heading out into the countryside to tend their crops. They pass country folk riding in carts or leading horses and donkeys laden with produce heading for market. The carts make a terrific din as they rumble down the narrow streets, the noise echoing off the walls of the tall buildings.

The smell of fresh bread fills the air as the bakers mould their dough. Breakfast is normally taken between nine and ten o'clock. This is a simple meal, consisting of bread, jam and fruit. By now, the streets are alive with the sound of hawkers selling their wares. Already, in the markets, prospective purchasers are waiting with eager anticipation for the fishmongers and poultry vendors to finish setting out their stalls.

The clerks and secretaries who run the administration of government are heading for the Palazzo della Signoria where their bosses live and work. Any official, dressed in the traditional red or black gown, known as the *lucco*, is likely to be buttonholed by locals who are hoping that they will put in a good word on their behalf with the Priors upstairs. A servant hurries through the square bearing the prize cuts of veal that have been reserved for the Priors' table. The more important merchants call for the first clients waiting patiently outside to be brought into their palaces. Artisans in their smocks and pointed caps settle down for the day's business.

Not everyone is hard at work. In doorways young men are playing cards, chess and dice. Others are taking part in more energetic games in the street, such as *civettino* (little owl), in which two contestants, stripped down to their shirtsleeves and leggings, deflect each other's playful punches. If there is a football game out at the stadium by the Porta al Prato to the east, you can hear the fans shouting on their favourite team. In fashionable via Tornabuoni a few young swells parade in their high-necked doublets, silk sleeves and finely tailored velvet hose designed to show their figures off to best advantage, eyed up by a smattering of pickpockets.

A group of elegant young Florentines – even the youngest boy is dressed in the height of fashion.

If you hear someone ringing a bell, it may be a beggar asking for alms. Although there is a terrible stench in many streets – the pungent aroma of horse dung mixed with straw and dust – many Florentines like to work with their doors open. As you pass their doorways, you will catch glimpses of their varied lives: a weaver working his loom, a carpenter chiselling a piece of furniture, or a tailor measuring up a velvet suit. A barber, who is shaving a prosperous lawyer under a portico, pauses as a mounted herald rides past, calling out the news that there will be a major tournament in Piazza Santa Croce in a few days.

Many workers stop for refreshment at popular taverns such as the well-known hostelry founded by Lorenzo de' Medici at Porta da San Gallo, on the north side of town. In summer they devour cold meats, zucchini flowers and vegetable jams, and in winter cured hams, spiced pies and broth. If you cross the Arno, you can admire the hive of industry on the banks with workers washing wool and tanners curing hides, but if you're squeamish don't look down into the water: it is completely discoloured by a mixture of refuse, sewage, animals' entrails, soap, tannin and various dyes.

As the afternoon wanes, shops begin to shut for the night, and workmen head home for the evening meal. This is a more elaborate affair than breakfast. The staple diet is pasta, with a salad to start, followed by meat (perhaps a small

A scene of debauchery in a tavern with a servant passing flagons of wine to customers upstairs who readily consume them.

pigeon or boiled kid) and then goat's milk cheese or fruit to finish. Richer families occasionally treat themselves to more exotic dishes such as a peacock followed by coloured jellies made of almond milk and flavoured with saffron. Most are not great topers, but there is always a glass of Vernaccia or Trebbiano wine to wash down the meal. Artisans have to make do with bread, onions and garlic, or a bowl of beans and a salad – they can only afford meat on feast days (of which there are a great many, fortunately). Most do not even possess a fork.

If you venture forth after the great bell in the tower of the Palazzo della Signoria has sounded the curfew, you will notice a different class has appeared on the streets. There are many insalubrious areas that you will learn to avoid. You will always see a throng of high-spirited Florentines heading for the most popular taverns where they can eat and drink to their hearts' content. Many of these taverns serve as brothels, and their names leave little to the imagination: Chiassolino (little whorehouse), where the cooks pimp for prostitutes, both male and female; Malvagia, whose name means both 'wicked woman' and 'ugly whore'; and Bertuccie and Fico, whose names ostensibly mean 'monkey' and 'fig' respectively, but in fact are both references to a part of the female anatomy (you can guess which). They are based either in the main shopping area around the Old Market, the public baths at San Michele Berteldi and, ironically, the archbishop's palace, or in the seamy area south of the Palazzo della Signoria.

The government tries hard to clamp down on prostitution, ordering the ladies of the night to wear gloves, bells and high-heeled slippers, but to little avail. It has certainly failed to deter the hard-bitten professionals who frequent the taverns near the Faenza gate where the German and Flemish weavers like to drink. The banks of the Arno are also havens of vice, resounding with the sounds of high-spirited men gambling at cards and dice.

SHOPS AND MARKETS

There are many shops between the Piazza della Signoria and the Old Market. The shops and workshops (known as *botteghe*) of each individual trade tend to be located close together. There are estimated to be as many as 270 *botteghe* for the wool trade alone in the city. Via Calimala, opening onto the Old Market, is filled with clothes shops. Round the corner you can indulge your fancy for silks and brocades in the shops on via Vacchereccia, Por Santa Maria and Porta Rossa. Por Santa Maria, approaching the Ponte Vecchio, also houses bankers and goldsmiths, who produce an astonishing range of beautifully crafted work including rings, enamels, precious metals, altar-frontals, chalices, book covers and leather boxes.

Once there [by the Baptistery] bear to the right a few paces... and ask for the Mercato Vecchio. There halfway down the street stands a happy whorehouse which you will know by the very smell of the place. Enter and give my greetings to the whores and madams...the blonde Helena and the sweet Matilda will greet you... You will see Giannetta and... the naked and painted breasts of Claudia... Here...you can find anything that is illicit.

IL PANORMITA

The Old Market is a hive of activity with Florentines buying and selling food – on the column in the centre stands Donatello's statue of Abundance.

Shoemakers are tucked away in Chiasso Baroncelli off Piazza della Signoria. Cap and hatmakers operate from Piazza de' Brunelleschi and via dei Rigattieri alongside the rag trade, whose shops contain a hotchpotch of cushions, mattresses, chests, horse covers and even discarded ecclesiastical cowls and cassocks. There is a raffish feel to this area. Second-hand clothes dealers and pawnbrokers are based here and are happy to accept anything of value. However, don't ask too many questions about where their goods have come from: a good proportion of it is reputed to have been stolen. A little further out, around Santa Maria Novella, you will find embroiderers, while across the river, around Piazza Santo Spirito, are goldsmiths, carpenters, silversmiths and cabinet-makers. Wool- and leather-workers prefer the Santa Croce area. On the Ponte Vecchio your senses will be assaulted by the shops of butchers, grocers, bakers, mercers, hosiers, coopers and metalworkers.

If you prefer to shop in relative peace and quiet, head across Piazza della Signoria towards the Badia, where you will find stationers or booksellers in via dei Librai and via dei Cartolai, based near the centre of government (appropriately, considering the amount of paperwork they generate). Vespasiano de Bisticci used to run the most interesting bookshop in Italy here, with a wide selection of ancient manuscripts and top-quality maps, the latter a speciality of Florence. There has been a stream of seafarers asking to see a map by Paolo Toscanelli, who made his name by creating the gnomon (a device for calculating the sun's altitude from its shadow) that runs down the nave of the Cathedral, and who made the revolutionary claim that there is a route through the western ocean to Asia. This has caused much excitement and a Genoese explorer called Cristoforo Colombo has studied Toscanelli's map and is currently attempting to find financial backing in Spain or Portugal to test his thesis. Amerigo Vespucci, an ambitious partner of a firm run by Giannetto Berardi, agents for the Medici bank in Spain, is reputed to be heading for Seville to see what profits might be made from financing an Atlantic expedition.

There are two major markets in the city centre. Beneath the elegant, airy loggias of the Old Market (Mercato Vecchio) there is a cacophony of sights and smells as vendors vie with one another to sell their goods. If you are feeling hungry, you can take a slice of roast pork from a spit, or a piece of stewed eel from a fishmonger, though the fish is fresher round the corner on via Peciaiuoli near the Ponte Vecchio. A vegetable vendor will offer you a piece of watermelon from Pistoia, known as *brucia Pistoia* ('Pistoia's burning', due to its red colour). On the steps of churches on the four corners of the square beggars ask for alms. The market is full of women eyeing up the produce – the grandest Florentine matron is as adept

at haggling over a brace of capons as the lowliest artisan's wife. If it has been raining and the ground is muddy, these matrons tend to wear cloth slippers in wooden clogs, with platform soles.

You can escape the din and aroma of meat and fish by going round the corner to the New Market (Mercato Nuovo), where the money-changers and dealers in silks and textiles go about their business in a more subdued atmosphere. They lay out their purses and ledgers on a green cloth-draped over a table, and the dominant sound is the click-clack of abacus beads as they work out the best deal.

THE PUBLIC ROLE OF WOMEN

There is big divide between the public roles of upper- and lower-class Florentine women. In the markets you will

A charming, demure girl in a gold embroidered brocade dress gazes out of Ghirlandaio's fresco (see Plate IV).

see all classes of women doing their shopping. Elsewhere, however, it is mostly working-class women you will see in the streets since few of them work at home. Some are in domestic service, acting as wet-nurses; others spin wool, sell linen, make female clothing or work in taverns. In contrast, more privileged women spend the vast majority of their time at home. They have no vote and are banned from participating in politics or joining religious processions, though you will see them leaning from a window to enjoy the excitements of Carnival.

When the grander ladies do appear in public, they make sure they are suitably dressed in flowing silk dresses trimmed with gold, a tight bodice and high neckline. On their feet, if it is fine weather, they wear leather slippers. Their skin is a fashionably pale colour, caused by the application of sulphur, which accentuates their expensive jewelry. Florentine men like their women to show off their beauty. Lorenzo de' Medici is a typical example, waxing lyrical over his current mistress Nencia da Barberino's damask bodice, her necklace of red links with a pendant, and the gold belt around her skirt that spreads out when she kneels in church.

COURTESANS

If you attend a service in church, you will most likely see a number of strik-ing, well-dressed ladies who appear to take their devotions seriously, even if the sermon is terribly boring and their neighbours are half asleep. But look more carefully. The way that a certain lady's hair is done, with a couple of golden curls escaping from her headpiece, the careful arrangement of her shawl so that it both covers and draws attention to the swell of her bosom, and her look, fixed on the altar and yet aware of all around her, all indicate that she may not be what she appears at first sight. When you leave the church, she may take longer to leave the piazza than is strictly necessary and you may see one or two circumspect men leaving a message with her servant. This demure lady is very likely a courtesan who uses church as a way to display her wares. If you are tempted to make an assignation yourself, be prepared. A Florentine courtesan is a highly educated lady who is as happy to discuss Petrarch's sonnets, sing arias or play the lute as she is to display her sexual proficiency in the bedchamber. And she will make a heavy charge for you to have the excitement of sampling the full range of her skills.

The Church strongly disapproves of the way that courtesans use church as a business opportunity, particularly as this has proved such a success. This is one of the reasons why men are segregated from women in many churches, including the Cathedral, which has a rood screen or a curtain of coarse cloth separating the two sexes. This tends to be seen as symbolical, the area for the women being the left-hand or 'sinister' side.

SCHOOL AND UNIVERSITY

The fame of Florentine teachers is spreading and many now send their children here to share their wisdom. Students must be prepared to work hard, however. Florentines send their children to school at the age of seven. A few of the grandest families, such as the Medici, Strozzi and Gondi, employ private tutors, but many foreigners now send their children to one of the schools scattered all over the city. One of the best is next to Orsanmichele. Many of the leading humanists follow

The serious business of learning grammar, as depicted by Andrea Pisano in one of his reliefs for the Cathedral campanile.

the lead set by Niccolo da Uzzano, a statesman at the beginning of the century, and endow scholarships for poor provincial students.

Education used to have a purely practical end, a way of learning to count and express oneself, the two key factors in running a business. Young boys learnt to answer questions such as how many bales of cotton would be needed to make a bolt of cloth. The main subjects were grammar and arithmetic. Girls, on the other hand, were encouraged to learn every aspect of life in the household.

This is all changing, however, and a whole new syllabus has evolved. Alongside grammar and arithmetic pupils learn rhetoric, geometry and music. The art of rhetoric is valued very highly, since it may lead you to become a famous orator. Florentines still hold in awe their fellow countryman Gianozzo Manetti for delivering a two-hour oration in Latin to King Alfonso of Aragon, who listened so intently that he never noticed the fly on the end of his nose.

Many of the best schoolmasters call themselves humanists and are passionately interested in the ancient world. Their pupils spend much of their time learning Latin, particularly the works of Ovid and Plutarch. The more sophisticated Florentines feel that giving their children a classical education adds lustre to their wealth, and they remember that Leonardo Bruni and Collucio Salutati, both chancellors of the republic earlier in the century, were noted humanists. Levels of literacy are very high. In between the hours of study, pupils are encouraged to take exercise, playing football, running, jumping and wrestling.

Nevertheless, not all teachers are up to scratch and there are all sorts of jokes about the pedantic schoolmaster, with his weak memory, clumsy tongue and dull intellect, dressed in his bonnet and threadbare gown, complaining of indigestion, eyestrain and backache. Some take advantage of their charges: only recently the tutor Rafaello Canacci was accused by Ludovico Buonarotti of making advances to his son Lionardo, brother of the gifted Michelangelo. He was found guilty, fined 20 florins, and given a suspended prison sentence.

At Florence University there is a clearly defined hierarchy with masters of civil law at the top. A few years ago it was reckoned that they were earning an average of 440 florins, while those teaching rhetoric and poetry were on 330 florins, masters of canon law and medicine 300 florins, and basic grammarians 120 florins. There is a large scope to many subjects so that the study of stars includes astrology as well as astronomy, just as the study of minerals includes both alchemy and chemistry. There is no set age for students to enter university, and some are just fifteen years old.

Lorenzo has encouraged the study of law, medicine and theology at Pisa

A professor, seated at his desk, delivers a lecture to his students – whose minds seem to be on other matters.

University, partly because he wants clever lawyers and theologians out of the way. He remembers the trouble his grandfather had with the disagreeable Francesco Filelfo, whose *Book of Exile* vilified the Medici as usurers and promoters of vice, though Filelfo ended up as professor at Florence University.

Printing is still a novelty in Florence, with the first printed book less than twenty years old. It is a fascinating experience to watch the complexity of a printing press – the way that the movable letters are swiftly arranged in any amount of variations to produce different words. This is a

I this portrait by Machietti, Lorenzo de' Medici is
 wearing a scarlet lucco and holding a letter in
 right hand. He is portrayed as the virtual ruler
lorence, which can be seen over his shoulder.

II (Following pages) This view of Florence shows
the Cathedral and Palazzo della Signoria towering
above the other buildings. Note the city's stout
fortifications, and the four bridges crossing the Arno.

III (Above) *A typical Florentine palazzo interior –
in this case of the Palazzo Davanzati – with
brightly coloured walls and a massive fireplace.*
IV (Below) *Ghirlandaio sets the birth of John the*
*Baptist in the sort of bedroom only the wealthiest
families can afford. The scene is witnessed by
splendidly dressed women of the Tornabuoni
family and a maid bearing a basket of fruit.*

The famous
condottiere *Federico
da Montefeltro*,
dressed in armour
and attended by his
son, reads a book
in the study of his
palace. On his left leg
he proudly displays
the English Order
of the Garter.

Judging by the beauty of this portrait of Ginevra de' Benci, you can see why Leonardo da Vinci is the most sought-after artist in Italy.

VII *Botticelli gazes quizzically at the spectator in this detail of his* Adoration of the Magi.

VIII (Following page) *Dante, holding a copy of the* Divine Comedy, *stands outside the walls of his native city. The artist has taken the liberty of placing him beside Brunelleschi's dome, not built until a century after the poet's death.*

eally amazing development and will oon put all those monks, laboriously opying out ancient texts with their nest goose quills, out of business. ou can visit a press in via Calimala, r just out of town at the convent of an Jacopo di Ripoli. As you might xpect, the latter produces religious ooks – hymns, ballads and religious roadsheets – though it also prints latonic dialogues, showing a commendable broadmindedness.

FORBIDDEN LOVE

We're happy youths without a care, and o that we can satisfy our desires to the ull, we don't ever want to take a wife. Ie who isn't married can always do the om, ba, ba.

ANTONFRANCESCO GRAZZINI

Regarding someone who had been a ood-looking boy and later was a handome man, this was too great an affront, ince when young he lured husbands way from their wives, and now he lures vives away from their husbands.

NICCOLÒ MACHIAVELLI ON A JOKE
BY CASTRUCCIO CASTRACANI

f you are out late in the evening and ou come across a group of boisterus young men, watch out. They are robably up to no good. Florence has a eputation for homosexuality, at least n the opinion of the Officials of the Night (nicknamed by irreverent locals the office of buggers'), an organ of

government designed to clamp down on this vice. For the last half century it has been prosecuting young men accused of sodomy. Actually, it offers immunity from prosecution for those who turn themselves in. There seem to be no shortage of candidates; every year some 400 are implicated and about forty are condemned to a variety of punishments. This is normally a fine or some form of ritual shaming: a stint in the pillory, a flogging through the streets (often riding an ass, the traditional sign of ignominy) or at the column in the Old Market. Sometimes the luckless man is forced to wear a fool's cap with the epithet *sodomita* or the letter B, standing for *buggerone*. Recently, two men were compelled to process naked through the streets carrying a candle, to the church of Santissima Annunziata.

Despite the threat of these punishments, homosexuality is still rife. Churches are often used for assignations, and dancing and fencing schools are well known as places where athletic young men meet after taking exercise. If you are crossing the Ponte Vecchio of an evening, you will see no shortage of handsome young men, dressed up in velvet and satin, heading for the Mazzanti brothers' butcher's shop. A less decorous and distinctly rougher crowd can be found in via dei Pellicciai, running from the Old Market to via Porta Rossa, or in the tavern of the Buco near Ponte Vecchio. This is where older men engage in a nightly hunt to steal hats or caps off young men, which they regard as licence to commit sodomy. If you find all this too unpalatable, you can make an anonymous denunciation in one of the boxes on the outside of the Cathedral, the church of San Piero Scheraggio or Orsanmichele.

JUSTICE

Proud, greedy, traitor, liar, lustful, ungrateful, full of deceits, I am Bonaccorso di Lapo Giovanni.

INSCRIPTION BENEATH AN EXECUTED CRIMINAL
IN THE PALAZZO DELLA PODESTÀ

You would be well advised not to do anything illegal while you are in Florence. There seems to be no end of different organs of justice, and before you have spent many days in the city, you are likely to come across the authorities pursuing a malefactor, a prostitute being flogged, or even a condemned man being executed on a scaffold. As a guide, monetary matters are normally dealt with by the court of the Cambio guild, while crimes such as blasphemy are addressed by the bishop's tribunal.

More serious crimes are dealt with by the Podestà, and anyone who passes through the forbidding door of its palace opposite the Badia is in deep trouble. He (or occasionally she) is greeted with defamatory murals on the walls of the courtyard showing criminals being punished for their sins, often being tortured by devils, with graphic inscriptions describing their crime to help them on their way to hell. A recent addition are Sandro Botticelli's portraits of the Pazzi conspirators with verses beneath added by Lorenzo de' Medici. Rumour has it that the favourite means of eliciting a confession from the accused is to apply the *strappado*, a truly terrible fate. The arms of the victim are first tied rigidly behind his back, then he is hoisted high and dropped again and again until his sinews tear, and his joints come out of their sockets. Then he is deemed ready to confess his crimes. You may see a survivor of this gruesome torture hobbling through the streets.

If you ask the locals about their justice system they will make no mention of this fearsome device, but prefer to dwell on how impartial their courts are. They will stress how every effort is made to keep judges and citizens apart to prevent bribery and collusion. The most important judges are non-Florentines who are given short terms of office, rarely as much as a year. The whole question of impartiality is a very sensitive one so be careful if you find yourself holding a conversation on the subject. In theory, the grandest families are treated in the same way as the poorest citizen; in practice, there is one law for the rich and another for the poor. You may also come across exiles, of whom there are quite a number, in your travels across the rest of Tuscany. They will

ill your ears with tales of gross mis-carriages of justice, stories of grandees bribing officials, suborning witnesses, and even hiding until their relatives can have their sentences quashed.

WIT AND HUMOUR

First stop them using loaded dice.

COSIMO DE' MEDICI ON THE LAW
TO STOP PRIESTS GAMBLING

Florentines like nothing better than a good, lively discussion on any subject from high politics to the price of fish in the market. They have a reputation for caustic humour, love pithy expressions and delight in making fun of their neighbours. Above all Florentines, and Tuscans in general, enjoy puns – such as the Medici jester Matteo Franco running down his rival Luigi Pulci, describing him as a 'louse clinging to the Medici balls' (*pulci* meaning louse). The saying 'To deal with a Tuscan, you can't afford to be one-eyed' sums up their attitude to life. A Florentine relies on his own wit for 'he who transacts his own business does not soil his hands'. When Cosimo de' Medici was dying, his wife asked him why he was lying with his eyes shut, to which he replied: 'To train them.' Cosimo's dry, earthy humour is typical of the Florentines' dislike of pomposity. There was much amusement when the herald Filarete, who used to make declamations, was caught in *flagrante delicto* with a girl in the Palazzo della Signoria.

FLORENTINE MAXIMS

A melancholy fellow 'holds his soul back with his teeth'

A self-satisfied man is 'as heavy as macaroni water'

An irritable woman calls her husband an ass to which he retorts: 'If you were an ox instead of a cow, we should look well standing with the Holy Family by the manger'

'His faith is shorter than a hare's tail'

To bungle a business deal is 'to remain with dry teeth'

To complicate an issue is 'to look for five legs on a sheep'

To hate one's neighbour is 'to tear out his tongue by the neck'

Of credulous dupes they say 'in the good old days when goats wore clogs'

'A chaffinch in the hand is worth a thrush in the bush'

Someone not repaid for his efforts is 'like the donkey who carries wine and drinks water'

When happy, one says 'It's raining caresses'

If hesitant, one is 'hovering on wings' or is 'picking one's brains'

If afraid, of losing time one says 'Don't think that I shall go away with my hands full of flies'

If someone is angry 'he puts his patience under his feet'

To do a useless job is 'to pour water in a mortar' or 'to wash bricks'

IV · POLITICIANS, PAINTERS, PHILOSOPHERS AND CONDOTTIERI

FLORENTINE POLITICS

You are hardly a man unless you have served in the Signoria at least once

FRANCESCO GUICCIARDINI

I've had more letters from would-be Priors than there are days in the year.

LORENZO DE' MEDICI COMPLAINING OF AN
ELECTION TO THE SIGNORIA

If you engage a Florentine in conversation, you will soon find that he is obsessed with politics – sometimes it seems as though they are incapable of talking about anything else. But you will need to concentrate hard if you ask him how the system works, since it is unbelievably complicated. The Palazzo della Signoria (also called the Palazzo dei Priori), with the highest tower in the city, is the home of the government, known as the *Signoria* (town council). This is composed of eight Priors (two from each quarter of the city) and a Standard-Bearer of Justice, known as the *Gonfaloniere*. They meet daily in the palace but are only in office for two months, so just when you have worked out who they all are they are replaced by a new cast of characters.

To make matters more complicated, they have advisers, known as the Twelve Good Men (*Buonomini*), who serve for three months, and sixteen standard-bearers from different areas (gonfalons) of the city who each serve for four months. In addition there are all sorts of committees with varying powers. The most important are the ten-man Committee of War, convened in times of emergency, and the eight

The fortified Palazzo della Signoria with its campanile is the centre of Florentine government.

[44]

man Security Committee, responsible for detecting and preventing crimes against the State.

Altogether, there is the incredible total of some 3,000 posts falling vacant and being refilled annually. To qualify for the three main offices, a man (never a woman) must be solvent and a member of a guild, and there must have been a gap of at least three years since he last served in office. The old feudal nobles are perceived to be a law unto themselves and are excluded. There is an extremely complex system of vetting who is eligible with three tiers: the first is a group of fifty members who select another group, the election secretaries (known as *accoppiatori*); they in turn scrutinize candidates for key offices. Names are drawn by lot from a purse, called a *borsa*.

The complexity of the system is designed to enable the leading families to control the top offices. They understand that the key to political control is to find out which names are placed in the *borsa*. And you will realize, after just a few days in the city, that when you mention the most important families in Florence, there is just one name on everyone's lips – the Medici. In fact, you can gain a better insight into Florentine politics by ignoring the activities in the Palazzo della Signoria altogether and concentrating instead on Lorenzo de' Medici. To understand the key role he plays in running Florence it helps to take a quick look at his family history.

THE MEDICI

If Florence was to have a tyrant, she could never have found a better or more delightful one.

FRANCESCO GUICCIARDINI
ON LORENZO DE' MEDICI

Lorenzo was a man endowed by nature, training, and practice with such enormous ingenuity, that he was in no way inferior to his grandfather Cosimo... And I believe that being inspired by the magnitude of his ability, when he found our citizens timid and of a servile spirit...he resolved to transfer to himself all public dignity, power, and authority, and in the end, like Julius Caesar, to make himself lord of the republic.

ALAMANNO RINUCCINI

Much has already been said of the Medici in this book, and anyone wanting to understand present-day Florence will find it very useful to have a basic knowledge of Medici history. The family are not particularly ancient (despite their claims to the contrary), but their rise to power has been spectacular. The key to their success has been the way they have used the vast profits from the family bank, just under one hundred years old, to buy political power. This is all done with great subtlety. The leading members serve on the various committees, but no more than other families. Lorenzo's grandfather Cosimo, whom he takes as a role model, served as *Gonfaloniere*

A LOAD OF BALLS

Everywhere you go in Florence, you will see the Medici *palle* (balls) prominently displayed on public buildings.

The Medici, anxious to emphasize their pedigree, proclaim that they are cannon balls or dents made by a giant in a shield held by a gallant Medici ancestor who promptly slew him.

There are two less flattering views of the balls' origin:

One is that the *palle* are actually coins, referring to the Medici's role as pawnbrokers, a distinctly less glamorous role and one the family is anxious to gloss over.

A more likely theory is that the *palle* are doctor's pills and refer to the family's origin as medics, hence Medici.

The *palle* are ubiquitous – in fact they have largely replaced the traditional Florentine symbols of the lily and the lion. But if you want to discuss their origin, be careful – Medici supporters are very touchy on the subject.

Lorenzo is equally cunning. He has manipulated the system to serve his own ends and extended the duration and powers of the emergency committees, known as the *Balie*, which he can pack with his own supporters. Just to make sure, key votes are carried out by hand, rather than by lot, so anyone who dares to vote against a Medici supporter has to do so publicly, and take the consequences.

Foreign princes treat Lorenzo, despite his protestations to the contrary, as a head of state and send their ambassadors straight to the Palazzo Medici, an imposing building in the centre of town. The most fortunate will be invited to stay. If so, they will be in good company. Some Florentines can still remember how Lorenzo's grandfather Cosimo entertained the Pope and the Byzantine Emperor here during the Council of Florence in 1439. Certainly, when the Pazzi recently tried to overthrow the government (see below), their key goal was to kill the two leading Medici, Lorenzo and his brother Giuliano.

THE PAZZI CONSPIRACY

Although this took place twelve years ago, its ramifications are still being felt in Florence. The Pazzi, an eminent banking family like the Medici, very nearly succeeded in overthrowing their bitter rivals. Lorenzo's brother Giuliano was stabbed to death before the high altar in the Cathedral on Easter

three times, but understood that true power lay in controlling his fellow citizens' purse strings. The best way to do this was through the Committee of Public Debt which scrutinized the finances of all those standing for public office. Cosimo therefore had the means to pressurize all those in his debt to ensure they voted for the Medici party.

A medal commemorating the Pazzi Conspiracy, showing the head of Giuliano de' Medici.

Sunday, 1478, and Lorenzo himself was wounded in the neck (a brave friend immediately sucked the wound in case the dagger had been poisoned). Archbishop Salviati, one of the main conspirators, only just failed to take the Palazzo della Signoria but the Priors, roused from their dinner and suspicious of his manner, locked themselves into the tower and sounded the tocsin.

Afterwards, Lorenzo wreaked terrible vengeance, executing most of the male members of the Pazzi family, along with the archbishop and the two priests who had attempted to kill him (their nose and ears were cut off first, to prolong their agony). He then ordered the removal of the Pazzi coat-of-arms from every building, and renamed streets bearing their name. Although Lorenzo is firmly in power,

he is still nervous of assassination and if you see him walking through the streets, wrapped in a purple cloak and hood, he is likely to be escorted by armed and cloaked attendants. They are a tough-looking band and live up to their nicknames Black Martin and Crooked Andrea (*Andrea Malfatto*), with a *bravo* from Pistoia called Garlic Saver (*Salvalaglio*) at their head wielding a naked sword.

MEET FAMOUS FLORENTINES

Florence harbours the greatest minds: whatever they undertake, they easily surpass all other men, whether they apply themselves to military or political affairs, to philosophy, or to merchandise.

LEONARDO BRUNI

It is now time to meet some of the main characters whom you may encounter on your walk round the streets. They are some of the most intelligent and talented men and women in Italy, and their fame has spread far and wide.

LORENZO DE' MEDICI (BORN 1450)

With a single gesture [Lorenzo] *was able to bend all the other citizens to his will.*

PIERO PARENTI

Lorenzo is now aged forty and has dominated Florentine politics for the past twenty-one years. A tall, dark figure, highly intelligent, with a retentive memory and a very good judge of character, his fellow citizens regard him with awe. His renowned charm and brilliance of conversation put all he meets at ease; they soon forget his ugly features, his flattened nose, his jutting lower jaw and his harsh and disagreeable voice. As the Venetian ambassador states: 'Before he begins to speak, his eyes speak for him.' Lorenzo is highly strung, with a facility for music, and has written some delightful poetry about his love of women and the countryside. His friendship and patronage of the leading artists, scholars and poets has given him the central role in the most brilliant cultural era in Florentine history, and earned him the title of 'the Magnificent' (*il Magnifico*). But Lorenzo's health is no longer robust, he suffers from asthma, gout and arthritis, and is now rarely seen indulging in his favourite past-times: riding out hawking on his favourite horse Morello or going to visit his villa, Poggio a Caiano.

FILIPPO STROZZI (BORN 1428)

Filippo is one of the richest men in Florence, yet another successful merchant-banker. He is one of the few leading Florentine nobles whom Lorenzo trusts and it was Filippo he sent to Naples in 1479 to talk to the treacherous King Ferrante before Lorenzo embarked on his audacious peace-making visit in the wake of the Pazzi Conspiracy. Filippo is also long-suffering. He is a great patron of the arts and commissioned Filippino Lippi just three years ago to paint a chapel in Santa Maria Novella only to find that Lorenzo, anxious to curry favour with Cardinal Carafa, recommended Lippi to go to work for him in Rome instead. Filippo accepted this with good grace, since he knows better than to fall out with Lorenzo and has even loaned him 9,000 florins recently. His ambition matches his great wealth and he has employed Bendetto da Maiano to build the grandest palace in the city on fashionable via Tornabuoni.

The façade of Palazzo Strozzi has been designed by Giuliano da Sangallo. Though not yet completed, it is already the grandest and most expensive in Florence.

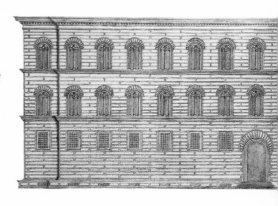

LEONARDO DA VINCI (BORN 1452)

I will lay before your Lordship my secret inventions, and then offer to carry them into execution at your pleasure...I can carry out sculpture in marble, bronze or clay, and also in painting I can do as well as any man.

LEONARDO'S LETTER OF RECOMMENDATION TO
LUDOVICO SFORZA, DUKE OF MILAN

Unfortunately, you are unlikely to meet Leonardo as he is based in Milan, but since he is the most brilliant Florentine alive, you ought to be prepared for a chance encounter on one of his visits back to his hometown. Leonardo is just two years younger than Lorenzo, and exerts a similar fascination on his fellow countrymen, but the two men are not close; Lorenzo has made no move to bring this most gifted fellow back to Florence – perhaps he is jealous. Leonardo, after all, is a self-made man, the illegitimate son of a notary and a peasant woman. He studied under the painter and sculptor Verrocchio but soon surpassed his master. Strikingly good-looking, a figure of grace and immense charm, Leonardo seems to enjoy his reputation for mystery and you won't meet anyone in Florence who really claims to understand him properly. He writes backwards so that his script is only decipherable in a mirror, designs fantastic machines that look as though they could fly or go underwater, and makes semi-miracu-

Leonardo da Vinci's knowledge of human anatomy – in this case the eye and brain – is incredible.

lous drawings of unborn babies and the cataclysmic forces of nature. Leonardo is the best living example of the idea that so appeals to Florentines, that man is the measure of all things; he is a *uomo universale*.

MARSILIO FICINO (BORN 1433)

Florence has produced some of the greatest Italian philosophers but their search for knowledge is a dangerous game. The grand old man of Florentine philosophy is Marsilio Ficino, tutor of Lorenzo de' Medici and head of the Florentine Academy. This centre of Neo-Platonism is an attempt to create a synthesis between Christianity and

In this bust, the leading philosopher Marsilio Ficino clutches a volume of his beloved Plato.

ancient Greek philosophy, notably the works of Plato. Marsilio has, in fact, translated the complete works of Plato into Latin. Lorenzo, one of his leading disciples, is a regular attendee at the Academy's annual banquet on 7 November celebrating Plato's birthday. Rather surprisingly Marsilio has also taken holy orders. He is a small man, five feet tall, with a big nose, a small chin and long, graceful hands. The Church is highly suspicious of his ideas and has attacked his study of astrology and magic. He is considered fortunate not to have been condemned for heresy.

PICO DELLA MIRANDOLA (BORN 1463)

This has been the fate of Marsilio's most brilliant pupil. A generation younger than his master, Pico is the leading philosopher in Florence and a great friend of Lorenzo. An aristocrat from a small province near Ferrara, Pico can read and write in Latin, Greek, Hebrew and Arabic. Slender and well-built, with striking good looks, he has had a complicated love life, and was wounded and thrown into prison after attempting to run off with a cousin of Lorenzo's; it is a measure of Pico's charm that the great man ordered his release himself. More recently Pico has been in trouble after publishing his *Theses*, an attempt to provide a synthesis of all philosophical systems, including magic and mysticism. Pico's provocative challenge to all comers to debate them has drawn down the wrath of the church authorities and the Pope himself has accused him of heresy. After fleeing to France to escape the papal inquisitors, he was arrested on the orders of Innocent VIII, before Lorenzo instigated his release; he is currently living quietly in a villa in Fiesole under Medici protection.

SANDRO BOTTICELLI (BORN 1444)

Sandro paints women as beautifully as any artist in Italy, which is saying something. A good-looking man, with a long, sensitive face, big, deep-set eyes, sensuous lips and a heavy jaw, he is rather shy in the company of women – surprisingly, since he spends so much time painting their naked bodies. Sandro, like so many others,

ARTISTS' NICKNAMES

Many leading artists have incredibly complicated names, hence their use of nicknames.

Botticelli (real name Alessandro di Mariano di Vanni Filipepi) has been given the nickname of 'little barrel' because of his rotund brother Giovanni.

Domenico di Tommaso Curradi di Doffo has adopted the name of 'garland-maker' (*ghirlandaio*) because he uses garland-like necklaces to enhance the beauty of his sitters.

Fra Angelico (Fra Giovanni da Fiesole) earned his nickname from his holy lifestyle, and the purity and serenity of his paintings.

Masaccio (Tommaso Cassai or Tommaso di Ser Giovanni di Monte) means 'fat', 'clumsy' or 'messy Tom' but belies the majestic paintings he executed in Florence.

Donatello (Donato di Niccolo di Betto Bardi), meaning 'little Donato', also gives little idea of his absolute mastery of the contrasting mediums of bronze and marble.

been spotted on several recent occasions attending services conducted by the fiery Savonarola who is strongly critical of portrayals of the nude. If you want to see one of his most beautiful paintings, you will have to go outside Florence (see p. 112).

DOMENICO GHIRLANDAIO (BORN 1449)

If you want your wife or your daughter painted, preferably clothed, Domenico Ghirlandaio is your man. Although he trained as a goldsmith, Domenico has devoted his career to painting and is now the most popular artist working in Florence. His fresco cycles in Santa Maria Novella and Santa Trinita are a must for every visitor to the city, and include marvellous portraits of all the most eminent Florentines, a very useful aide-mémoire in case you bump into them in the streets. In order to cope with the flood of commissions Domenico has assembled a large and well-organized studio. Its leading members are his brothers David and Benedetto, and his brother-in-law Sebastiano Mainardi.

GINEVRA DE' BENCI (BORN 1457)

Ginevra is a role model for all Florentine women, famed for her beauty and intelligence. An aristocratic lady with a rather austere reputation, she married Luigi Niccolini in 1474, and to celebrate this auspicious moment Leonardo da Vinci painted her

is deeply influenced by Neo-Platonism; one of its main concerns is the nature of beauty and Sandro has certainly succeeded magnificently in his paintings of Venus. The more religious-minded are scandalized by Sandro's willingness to use his beautiful models either as the Virgin clothed or as Venus naked. Perhaps he has taken these criticisms on board. Sandro is known to be deeply religious and has portrait, one of the few paintings he has made in his native city. Ginevra also appears in the celebrated fresco of the *Visitation* by Ghirlandaio in Santa Maria Novella.

CONDOTTIERI AND THE ART OF WARFARE

Thus the arms of Italy were either in the hands of lesser princes, or of men who possessed no state; for the minor princes did not adopt the practice of arms from any desire for glory, but for the acquisition of either property or safety. The others (those who possessed no state) being bred to arms from their infancy, were acquainted with no other art, and pursued war for emolument, or to confer honour on themselves.

NICCOLÒ MACHIAVELLI

War is a dangerous and risky business, interfering with trade and costing lives. The best way to wage it is to pay professionals to do the fighting on your behalf. That is the view of Florentines, and indeed Italians in general. There is no shortage of soldiers ready to do the fighting. Their leaders, known as *condottieri* (mercenary captains) are some of the most famous men of the age. Federico da Montefeltro, until recently commander of the Florentine army, was a prince in his own right, and has filled his beautiful palace in the hilltop town of Urbino with priceless works of art. To acquire the money to pay for all this, Federico

was prepared to be a ruthless warrior, and commanded the Florentine army when it brutally sacked Volterra on the orders of Lorenzo de' Medici in 1472, during a dispute over ownership of the lucrative alum mines. However, despite his close relationship with Lorenzo, Federico supported those behind the Pazzi Conspiracy.

This sums up the problem. *Condottieri* are unreliable, mercenaries who fight for money, who owe little allegiance to their employers, and who are liable to change sides. They may look the part, dressed in glittering armour and mounted on their warhorses, but are reluctant to risk their lives on the field of battle. For these *condottieri*, war is just a profitable way of making money. The alternative to using *condottieri* is to form a citizens' militia.

With Lorenzo de' Medici in charge, visitors feel perfectly safe when they arrive in Florence. The locals are often heard to comment that this is a wonderful moment to visit the city, during a prolonged period of peace. In fact, Lorenzo is worn out from his continual efforts to keep it this way. He is only too aware that warfare is a much more violent business outside Italy and that powerful foreign princes, such as Charles VIII of France and Ferdinand of Aragon, both of whom have claims to the kingdom of Naples, are casting covetous eyes on Italy. An invasion would leave Florence, with her relatively small army, very vulnerable.

V · MUST-SEE SIGHTS

This is an age of gold, which has brought back to life the almost extinct liberal disciplines of poetry, eloquence, painting, architecture, sculpture, music and singing to the Orphic Lyre. And all this in Florence!

MARSILIO FICINO

Florence is considered the finest and most beautiful city – not only in Christendom, but in the entire world.

GIOVANNI RUCELLAI

Florentines are only too happy to show you the chief sights in their city, of which they are immensely proud.

They feel that this a very auspicious moment to live in Florence and that the remarkable works of art created by their fellow citizens have made it a new Rome, rivalling the achievements of antiquity. Even the contracts for many of these buildings and works of art specify that they should be made 'as beautiful as possible' (*più bello che si può*).

THE CATHEDRAL

[Brunelleschi's dome] with its shadow covers all the Tuscan people.

ALBERTI, *DELLA PITTURA*

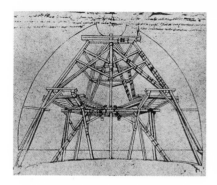

Even the scaffolding for Brunelleschi's grand dome was a masterpiece of engineering.

POPE EUGENIUS IV *So this is the little man who would be brave enough to turn the world on its axis?*

BRUNELLESCHI *Just give me a point, Your Holiness, where I can fix my lever, and I'll show you what I can do.*

The first place to see on your visit to Florence is the Piazza del Duomo. The three buildings facing onto the piazza – the Cathedral (known locally as the Duomo, though its real name is Santa Maria del Fiore), Baptistery and bell-tower (*campanile*) – form a magnificent ensemble. Florentines like to take their evening stroll, the *passegiata*, in this piazza, where they can exchange gossip. From wherever you are staying in Florence you will be able to see Filippo Brunelleschi's great dome on the Cathedral, which rises high above the surrounding buildings. It is a source of pride to all Florentines, and no wonder, for the problem of erecting a dome over the crossing (which is an

BRUNELLESCHI'S INGENUITY

Florentines revel in the many ingenious machines Brunelleschi invented during the construction. He even designed a café for the workers high up in the dome, to maximize the time they spent at work.

The most remarkable machine was an ox-hoist for lifting enormous blocks of stone hundreds of feet into the air. It consisted of a highly convoluted system of interconnecting wheels, gears and screws, with three drums made from an enormous and hardy elm tree, and ropes from Pisa over 600 feet long and weighing 1,000 pounds. The beauty of this infinitely complex machine, which even boasted a reverse gear, the first in the history of engineering, was that it required just one ox, the traditional beast of burden, to turn the shaft and set it in motion.

In total, it is estimated that the hoist lifted some 70 million tons of marble, stone, bricks and mortar during the construction of the dome.

incredible 138 feet wide) had seemed impossible until Brunelleschi found a solution. His design for the dome, so simple and yet so clever, consists of an inner and outer shell, giving both strength and lightness, while the ribs, linked by horizontal rings of brick-work, absorb the lateral thrust.

The achievement of building the dome was Brunelleschi's alone. He made this plain at the time, refusing to give credit to his co-architect Lorenzo Ghiberti. Florentines love to hear how he called Ghiberti's bluff by feigning illness so that his rival had to stop work, understanding nothing of Brunelleschi's complicated plans. Cosimo de' Medici, who greatly admired Brunelleschi, used his influence to persuade Pope Eugenius IV to consecrate the Cathedral in a splendid ceremony in 1436, after the work was finally completed. And it was from the doorway of the Cathedral that Brunelleschi rationalized a scheme of linear perspective composition with an empirical collection of paints, a panel and a mirror, using the Baptistery as his subject.

Florentines are superstitious and when lightning strikes the dome (which it frequently does) they worry that its great height, reaching to the heavens, has incited the wrath of God. Visitors who are not concerned by divine anger, and who have lots of energy, can climb up Brunelleschi's dome, which allows a fantastic view over the rooftops of Florence and the surrounding hills.

You may be surprised to discover that several major works of art inside the Cathedral have violent associations, including a fresco of a famous mercenary leader (*condottiero*). Paolo Uccello depicted Sir John Hawkwood as an imposing general, mounted on his warhorse, based on the antique prototype of Fabius Maximus, the Roman general who defied Hannibal. But appearances are deceptive and even a century after his death those with long memories still shudder at the mention of Hawkwood's name. He was a brutal Englishman, one of the most ferocious of all *condottieri*, whose marauding

There is no controlling Donatello's unruly children as they run round the Cathedral's choir loft.

White Company left a dreadful swathe of destruction as it looted and pillaged its way round France and northern Italy. Hawkwood's soldiers specialized in attacking towns by night. Once inside the walls, they would kill the men, rape the women, and create complete mayhem. No wonder the Florentines were so keen to pay the ruthless Englishman to fight on their side.

Near the high altar are two choir lofts (*cantorie*) with sculptures by Donatello and Luca della Robbia of children behaving in typical Italian fashion, dashing about with complete abandon and blowing trumpets for all their worth. These sculptures witnessed one of the most dramatic moments in recent history, the bloody climax of the Pazzi Conspiracy on Easter Sunday, 1478 (see p. 46).

THE CAMPANILE AND BAPTISTERY

Speak, speak or be damned!

DONATELLO ADDRESSING HIS STATUE OF HABAKKUK

To me was conceded the palm of victory by all the experts and by all those who competed with me. Universally I was conceded the glory without exception.

GHIBERTI'S EXPLANATION OF
THE COMPETITION IN HIS *COMENTARII*

Outside the Cathedral stands the campanile. With an absolute belief in talent, it was assumed that the gifted painter Giotto must be a good archi-

The two finalists in the competition for the Baptistery doors – do you prefer the Sacrifice of Isaac *by Brunelleschi (above) or Ghiberti (below)?*

tect as well, and he was awarded the job of designing it in 1334. The *Prophets* sculpted by Donatello for the niches on the exterior are so realistic that passing locals greet the bald-headed figure of Habakkuk, known affectiontely as 'pumpkin-head' (*lo Zuccone*), s an old friend.

Next to the Cathedral is the Baptistery. If you ask a local about the history of the building, he will proudly tell you that it is a converted ancient Roman temple of Mars and that it contains a relic of the True Cross given by the Emperor Charlemagne. But what he will really enjoy is the chance to recall the feud between Ghiberti and Brunelleschi. This originated in the competition for a second set of bronze doors for the Baptistery in the winter of 1400–1. When Ghiberti narrowly won the competition, the more experienced Brunelleschi, incensed at the verdict, turned his back on his career as a sculptor and took up architecture instead.

PIAZZA DELLA SIGNORIA

Whoever holds sway over the piazza always controls the city.

GIOVANNI CAVALCANTI

They did not show much spirit, for if they had been really interested in money, they could have had 10,000 or more.

COSIMO DE' MEDICI ON BRIBING HIS
JAILOR WITH 1,800 FLORINS
TO OBTAIN HIS FREEDOM

The Piazza della Signoria is the hub of civic life. Thieves know that there are rich pickings to be had in this square, so be on your guard. If you are lucky you may also see one of the jousts or mock battles that are held on special occasions in the piazza. Locals still remember how the crowd went wild when a mare in season was let loose among a group of stallions. Two lions used to be kept in a cage in the piazza, highly appropriate as the lion is the heraldic emblem of the city. In July 1331 there was much excitement when a lioness gave birth to two cubs, which Florentines regarded as a highly favourable omen for the city.

The lions are now housed within the rugged and imposing bulk of the Palazzo della Signoria, built by Arnolfo di Cambio. The Palazzo della Signoria is the town hall and has been the centre of government since the beginning of the last century (it is also sometimes confusingly called the Palazzo del Popolo, Palazzo dei Priori and Palazzo Ducale, reflecting its changing use). The Medici have an ambivalent relationship with the palace. Cosimo the Elder hated the place, never forgetting the months he spent imprisoned here in 1433 in a little cell high up in the tower. He was so fearful of being poisoned that he scarcely ate anything, but managed to bribe the government into releasing him on condition that he went into exile. On his return, he immediately transferred power to his own home.

On the outside of the Palazzo della Signoria stands an L-shaped platform, where orators speak, hence its name the *ringhiera* (haranguing-place). This

SYMBOL OF THE CITY

In 1501 the fledgling Florentine
Republic will commission from
Michelangelo the colossal marble
statue of David.
This heroic 17-foot high nude statue
is instantly adopted by Florentines
as a symbol of their city.
In 1504 the statue is taken from the
Cathedral workshop; forty men
take four days to pull it through the
streets to the piazza where it is placed
outside the Palazzo della Signoria.
The gigantic statue arouses an
almost superstitious feeling among
the citizens and acts as a symbolic
guardian against the
republic's enemies.

is where the Priors take their oath of
office, where proclamations are read
out and where foreign dignitaries are
received. When the Turkish ambassador presented his credentials recently,
Florentines were astonished at the lion
and giraffe he brought as gifts, though
the unfortunate giraffe, unaware of
the ungiving nature of Florentine
architecture, soon died when it hit its
head on the lintel of a door.

The *ringhiera* is also used for important religious events, and you may
well see Florentines attending a mass
here, listening to a sermon or admiring a display of particularly holy
relics. If you want to watch a review of
Florentine troops, plus have a chance
of seeing leading government officials

(and maybe even Lorenzo de' Medici
himself), go to the handsome Loggia
della Signoria next door. This is occasionally used for executions, and is
where declarations of war and peace
are made. On the far side of the square
eminent lawyers can often be seen
emerging from the Palazzo del Tribunale di Mercanzia, the courthouse
for all commercial disputes among
Florentine merchants.

If you want to see inside the Palazzo
della Signoria you must push your way
past the crowd of political hangers-
on and all those who have come to
pay their taxes to gain admittance
to the building. Many of the most
important rooms have recently been
decorated with splendid frescoes of
Roman statesmen by Domenico Ghirlandaio and the *Labours of Hercule*
by the brothers Antonio and Piero de
Pollaiuolo in the Sala dei Gigli – a
worthy subjects but rather hard-going.
Some cynics say that Lorenzo has
deliberately promoted this splendid
decoration to disguise the fact that the
palace is no longer a centre of power,
which has passed to him.

At the top of the palace's 308-foot
high tower hangs the great bell known
as *la Vacca* (the cow), due to its low
mooing sound. When Florentines hear
its ringing, they know there is a crisis
and congregate in the piazza. At this
mass meeting (*parlamento*) decisions
are taken by a show of hands.

ORSANMICHELE

There are always crowds of people thronging in the streets around the little church of Orsanmichele, a converted grainstore. They are normally members of the various guilds who have their headquarters in handsome palaces overlooking the church. You can watch these merchants and tradesmen hurry by the niches on the exterior of the church, just occasionally sparing a glance for the statues commissioned by the guilds to promote their particular trade. Donatello's St George, carved for the Guild of Armourers, seems incredibly lifelike, staring out into the distance, dressed in full armour and gripping a spear that protrudes right into the street. The figure of John the Baptist is the work of Donatello's rival, Ghiberti. A work of technical wizardry, this was the first life-size bronze figure to be cast in 1,500 years.

More recently Verrocchio added to the collection with his beautiful group of Christ and St Thomas, paid for by Lorenzo de' Medici, a keen supporter of the cult of St Thomas. Verrocchio, who died just a couple of years ago, was an excellent painter as well as a sculptor but was reputed to have given up paint-

Donatello's remarkably lifelike statue of St George at the church of Orsanmichele.

MARBLE AND BRONZE

Florentine sculptors are equally adept in the use of marble and bronze. Both materials make great demands on the sculptor. When carving a piece of marble from the quarries of Carrara, the sculptor can't afford to make a single mistake or he may ruin the block.

Casting bronze with the 'lost wax' process, on the other hand, is immensely complex and dangerous, involving heating a mould to an incredibly high temperature until the wax melts and the bronze can be poured in. If a patron commissions a work in bronze, he will be proclaiming his wealth, since it is ten times more expensive than marble.

ing after seeing the beauty of an angel painted by his star pupil, Leonardo da Vinci. The group made a big impact on visiting Venetians and Verrocchio received an important commission from the Venetian Republic to sculpt an equestrian statue of the *condottiere* Bartolomeo Colleoni. If you have a spare minute, go inside Orsanmichele and admire the wonderfully ornate tabernacle by Andrea Orcagna, constructed immediately after Florence had been devastated by the Black Death.

PALAZZO STROZZI
AND SANTA TRINITA

I have heard about the elaborate preparations you have made with regard to the construction of that magnificent house, from which I have received the greatest pleasure, as much to hear of our prosperous condition, as to fix my attention on those things which concern the honour and glory of yourself, and in particular of all the family.

ROBERTO STROZZI TO HIS KINSMAN FILIPPO

And all this time they were demolishing the houses ... so that all the streets round were filled with heaps of stone and rubbish ... making it difficult for anyone to pass along. We shopkeepers were continually annoyed by the dust and the crowds of people who collected to look on, and those who could not pass with their beast of burden.

LUCA LANDUCCI ON THE BUILDING OF PALAZZO
STROZZI, 20 AUGUST 1489

If you want to see some of the richest and most glamorous figures in Florence, dressed in their finest clothes, head for via Tornabuoni, with all its tempting shops. You may catch a glimpse of the wealthy banker Filippo Strozzi emerging from his palace, which he intends to be the grandest in the city (if it is ever finished), or entering the church of Santa Trinita, where his family has a beautiful chapel. Leaving nothing to chance, Filippo invited a well-known astrologer and the archbishop of Florence to partake in the palace's dedication ceremony, which took place on 6 August just last year.

The Strozzi family are all united in singing Filippo's praises, taking pride in this ostentatious magnificence, and a horse tethered to one of the handsome wrought-iron rings on the façade may well be one of Strozzi's country cousins come to take an admiring look. There is some grumbling among the local residents about the mess that the workmen are making here, but Filippo has done his best to win critics over, enlarging via Tornabuoni and paying for a new façade for the church of Santa Maria degli Ughi.

If you go into the church of Santa Trinita, just down via Tornabuoni towards the Arno, you will find more evidence of the ambitions of the Strozzi. In adjoining rooms in the sacristy there are two beautiful paintings commissioned by Filippo's

FLEMISH MASTERS

Ghirlandaio's altarpiece of the *Nativity* over the altar in Santa Trinita shows the influence of Flemish painting in the unidealized character of the shepherds, one of whom bears the painter's features. Like many fellow artists, Ghirlandaio was overwhelmed by the appearance of a large altarpiece by Hugo van der Goes in the church of Sant' Egidio, attached to the Hospital of Santa Maria Nuova. It is larger than life and sixteen men were needed to carry it from the San Frediano gate to Sant' Egidio when it arrived on 28 May 1483. Commissioned by Tommaso Portinari, director of the Medici bank in Bruges, this triptych depicts the *Adoration of the Shepherds*, with the kneeling donors in the side panels.

Florentine artists are amazed that this great altarpiece is by a Flemish artist of whom they have never heard. They particularly admire the realism of the figures, the shepherds rushing in to worship the Christ child, the rich symbolical allusions and the extraordinary detail. Portinari is a great champion of Flemish painting and is very proud of his portrait by Rogier van der Weyden which hangs in his palace. He should be very pleased with the reception of the triptych by van der Goes but, in fact, he is furious, since the ship he had hired to bring a second Flemish altarpiece, by Hans Memling, has been seized by Hanseatic merchants. Instead of holding pride of place in the chapel Portinari had paid for in the Badia in Fiesole, the altarpiece is now installed in Danzig Cathedral.

forebear Palla Strozzi earlier in the century. Fra Angelico's *Deposition* testifies to Palla's religious piety while the Magi and their attendants, smothered in gold leaf, in Gentile da Fabriano's *Adoration* show quite clearly the fabulous wealth of the Strozzi family. But perhaps Filippo should show some caution, since Palla, the richest man in Florence, aroused the envy of Cosimo de' Medici and ended his days in exile.

In a chapel in the north aisle of Santa Trinita you will find frescoes by Domenico Ghirlandaio, the most popular painter in town. These were commissioned by Francesco Sassetti, a senior member of the Medici bank (an indifferent banker but a good courtier, he once wrote obsequiously to Piero de' Medici: 'I am indeed yours, your creature, and with you in life as in death.'). Ghirlandaio has filled the frescoes with portraits of contemporary Florentines, with members of the Medici family well to the fore. Look for the portrait of Lorenzo, instantly recognizable from his long, flattened nose; Sassetti stands alongside, while Lorenzo's sons Piero, Giovanni and Giuliano with their tutor Angelo Poliziano emerge, like figures from a trapdoor, into Piazza Santa Trinita. They are just in time to witness a miracle: St Francis bringing the Spini boy back to life after he had fallen to his death from the family palace in Piazza Santa Trinita. Unfortunately, Sassetti's desire to show his devotion to the Medici cause did not help his finances, and he recently died after losing a considerable fortune when the Lyons branch of the bank collapsed.

SANTA MARIA NOVELLA

There are two principal things men do in this world: the first is to procreate, the second to build.

GIOVANNI RUCELLAI, *RICORDANZE*

The chapel, that is, the Capella Maggiore, of Santa Maria Novella was opened. Domenico del Ghirlandaio had painted it, at the order of Giovanni Tornabuoni. And the choir of carved wood was also made round the chapel. The painting alone cost 1,000 gold florins.

LUCA LANDUCCI, *DIARIO FIORENTINO*, 1490

A short walk to the north-west takes you to the great Dominican church of Santa Maria Novella. The church's façade is dominated by the name of its patron, Giovanni Rucellai, inscribed in large capital letters. As with the Palazzo Rucellai down the road (behind Santa Trinita), it was designed by Leon Battista Alberti. Originally famous for his prodigious athletic feats (he could jump over the heads of ten men in succession with his feet together and throw an apple right over Brunelleschi's dome), Alberti was an inventor who owned a chamber of optical illusions, a great classical

The much admired façade of Santa Maria Novella, one of the finest in Florence.

scholar and a writer on everything including painting, navigation, the breeding of horses and mathematics.

Rucellai was particularly proud of this façade, executed in the new classical style, because it was almost the only major church in Florence to possess one. Even the façade of the Medici church of San Lorenzo is just bare masonry. Inside the church the Rucellai have a family chapel, where a magnificent altarpiece by Duccio, the greatest Sienese artist, has been hanging for the past 200 years.

The Medici loom large in Santa Maria Novella. On the entrance wall of the church the parvenu Guasparre Lama, anxious to curry favour with the family, commissioned Botticelli to paint the *Adoration of the Magi* with portraits of leading members of his family (Botticelli has used this as an excuse to give himself star billing). Lorenzo was not taken in by Lama and he has been convicted for fraud by the Guild of Money-Changers.

Much to the annoyance of the Rucellai and the Strozzi familes, Giovanni Tornabuoni, another wealthy banker (and, more importantly, uncle of Lorenzo), has taken over the sanctuary, the plum site behind the high altar. Tornabuoni has commissioned Ghirlandaio to paint the walls with scenes from the lives of the Virgin and St John the Baptist, a job he has just completed for the sum of 1,000 florins. As at Santa Trinita, Ghirlandaio enjoys including his contemporaries in these biblical scenes. The painter himself, together with his brother, looks on calmly as Joachim (the Virgin's father) is expelled from the Temple, while Lorenzo's mother, Lucrezia Tornabuoni, sister of Giovanni, assists at the birth of St John the Baptist. Her female attendants are clothed in the most fashionable brocades and voided velvets embroidered with pearls and silver tinsel. Ghirlandaio had a number of assistants working on these frescoes. Tongues are already wagging that the most gifted of these, young Michelangelo Buonarotti, may one day surpass his master. Michelangelo is also a budding sculptor and has recently carved a statue to look like an antique. Connoisseurs can scarcely believe that it is not at least a thousand years old.

The wooden crucifix in the transept of the church was carved by Brunelleschi. He did this in a spirit of friendly rivalry with Donatello after he had described Donatello's sculpture of Christ in Santa Croce as looking like a peasant. When Donatello first saw Brunelleschi's statue, and realized that he had been completely surpassed, he was so amazed that he dropped his apron in which he was carrying home his lunch, breaking the eggs on the floor. Brunelleschi, much amused by his friend's reaction, said with a laugh: 'What's your plan, Donatello? How can we have lunch if you have spilled everything?'

Two paintings on the site have also been inspired by Brunelleschi's unrav-

Masaccio's fresco of the Trinity *in Santa Maria Novella has the grandeur of an ancient Roman temple.*

elling of the science of perspective: the fresco of the *Trinity* by Masaccio (the coffered ceiling of which may have been designed by the architect himself), and the fresco of the *Deluge* by Paolo Uccello in the *Chiostro Verde* (green cloister) beside the church. In this latter work Noah's Ark, seen in sharp perspective, rises above despairing figures grimly fighting for survival in the floodwater. Uccello was so fascinated by perspective that it is said that his wife was unable to persuade him to leave his drawings and come to bed.

The chapterhouse off the cloister is very splendid, with impressive frescoes depicting the *Triumph of the Church* with black-and-white dogs (representing the Dominicans, traditional defenders of the faith, a pun on the Latin *domini canes* – dogs of the Lord) tearing apart wolves (representing heretics). This is a highly suitable subject for the monks to contemplate when they meet here, not least since their order was the instigator of the terrifying Inquisition. At the foot of the staircase leading to a suite of grand apartments off the cloister stands Donatello's marble statue of *Marzocco*. This heraldic lion has watched some highly prestigious visitors pass by during the past 70 years, including two Popes (Martin V and Eugenius IV), the German Emperor Frederick III and King Christian of Denmark.

PALAZZO MEDICI

I finally arrived at the house of the mag nificent Cosimo, where there awaitec me a house so noteworthy in its ceilings the height of its walls, the fineness o the doors and windows, the numbers o rooms and reception halls, the decora tions of the studies, the number an quality of the books there, the pleas antness and purity of the gardens; ane likewise the tapestries with which it i decorated, the chests of incomparabl workmanship and inestimable value masterly works of sculpture and picture. of infinite kinds – and even of the mos exquisite silver. It is the most beautifu house I have ever seen.

GALEAZZO MARIA SFORZA TO HIS FATHER
THE DUKE OF MILAN

If you are interested in politics or in art, you must use your contacts to obtain access to the Palazzo Medici on via Larga. Cosimo the Elder built the family palace on this busy street on the route major processions take from the Cathedral to San Marco. Anxious not to appear ostentatious (ignoring the fact that twenty other dwelling: were demolished to make space for it), he invited Michelozzo to build his palace and rejected a more elaborate design by Brunelleschi, who destroyec his model in a rage.

You may be surprised that the palace has such a fortified appearance; in fact, it just shows how nervous Cosimc was of his fellow citizens despite his apparent stranglehold on power. The interior is really fascinating. It houses two of Donatello's finest sculptures, both acquired by Cosimo: his *David*, and *Judith and Holofernes*. The bronze *David*, which stands in the courtyard, is much admired, an idealized slightly smaller than life-size nude figure, lost in contemplation. The rather gruesome group of *Judith and Holofernes* (the Old Testament heroine is in the act of decapitating Holofernes), meanwhile, has been transformed into a fountain and stands in the garden.

At the back of the palace on the ground floor is Lorenzo's *camera*, which contains three paintings of the *Battle of San Romano* by Paolo Uccello. If you manage to see them, don't ask where they came from. The Bartolini-Salimbeni family were 'persuaded' to sell them to Lorenzo much against their wishes. He is reputed to have paid just 50 florins each for the three panels, though there is a rumour that he was so keen to 'acquire' them that he sent round a gang one night who broke into the palace and stole them.

If you manage to go upstairs you will find some of the most wonderful works of art in Florence. Flemish tapestries, priceless artworks and swords of damascene steel vie with reliefs by Donatello and paintings by Giotto, Fra Angelico and the Fleming Petrus Christus. Visiting princes, cardinals and foreign ambassadors all long to have the chance to inspect Lorenzo's

The imposing Palazzo Medici stands on via Larga, one of the main thoroughfares in Florence.

study, a lovely room with walls covered in inlaid wood, where his most prized objects are kept: antique curios, incised gems, rings, coins, medallions and other exquisite small objects, some of which are reputed to have cost as much as 500 florins. His library is of equal interest, containing some 1,000 precious books and manuscripts in sumptuous velvet and tooled leather bindings. The most valuable objects in the whole collection are a unicorn's horn valued at 6,000 florins and an ornately carved *tazza* that Cardinal Giovanni of Aragon, who was shown it recently by Lorenzo, thought worth 4,000 ducats (a ducat is worth more or less the same as a florin).

FRESCO PAINTING

All great Florentine painters from
Giotto onwards have been trained in
the art of fresco painting.
This is a highly complex technical
process, requiring careful preparation
of the plaster on the wall.
The artist must paint on it while
it is wet, hence the name *fresco* – fresh.

MICHELANGELO

Michelangelo will do much of his best
work in Florence for the Medici
at San Lorenzo.
His New Sacristy will contain
magnificent tombs to Giuliano, Duke
of Nemours, and Lorenzo, Duke of
Urbino, son and grandson respectively
of Lorenzo the Magnificent.
The tombs will be chiefly memorable
for the four monumental nude figures
of the times of day (Day and Night,
Dawn and Dusk), carved on the
two sarcophagi.
The Laurentian Library above the
cloister will be Michelangelo's most
important architectural project in
his native city, with a very dramatic
staircase tumbling from the reading
room into the vestibule.
Despite this patronage, Michelangelo
will supervise the fortifications to
defend the city against his chief patron
Pope Clement VII (nephew of Lorenzo)
and his supporters after the Medici
are expelled in 1527.

The most exquisite room in the
palace is the chapel, painted for Lorenzo's
father Piero by Benozzo Gozzoli
with scenes of the *Journey of the Magi*.
It resembles the fabulous procession
of the confraternity of the Magi (of
which Lorenzo is the head) that winds
its way through the neighbourhood
on the feast of Epiphany. Gozzoli
has depicted the main members of
the Medici family: Piero himself, his
sons Lorenzo and Giuliano (the latter
with a leopard perched behind him on
his horse), and the Byzantine Emperor
John Palaeologus, who had attended
the Council of Florence in 1439, a major
diplomatic triumph for the Medici.
The artist himself appears among
a group of men wearing red caps,
traditional Medici colours, his name
inscribed on his cap. No expense was
spared in the fresco – the sky is painted
in lapis lazuli, and the figures covered
in gold and silver leaf.

SAN LORENZO

Just round the corner from the Palazzo
Medici stands the church of San
Lorenzo, and if you've failed to catch
sight of Lorenzo at his palace, your
best chance of seeing him is to attend a
service here. The church was commissioned
from Brunelleschi by Lorenzo's
grandfather Cosimo; it is built
in the new style, based on the architect's
studies of ancient Roman buildings.
Cosimo also invited Donatello
to work in the family burial chapel in

he Old Sacristy and to sculpt bronze panels for the two pulpits, some of his most dramatic works. Lastly, Cosimo commissioned the reprobate Filippo Lippi to paint a beautiful altarpiece. When you look at the beauty of the Madonna, you would scarcely believe that she was, in fact, Lippi's wife Lucrezia Buti, whom he abducted from a convent in Prato and by whom he had two children, one of them the painter Filippino Lippi.

Filippo was famed for his libidinous desires. To prevent his amorous escapades, Cosimo de' Medici locked him into his room in Palazzo Medici, but the enterprising painter made ropes out of his sheets, climbed out of the window and went out on the town. Having tracked him down, Cosimo decided to give up the struggle, and gave Filippo his freedom. The artist responded by painting some of his most beautiful works for his patron.

CONVENT OF SAN MARCO

Certain portions of [Cosimo de' Medici's] wealth...had not been righteously gained...but, as [the monks'] lodging was inadequate, [Pope Eugenius] remarked to Cosimo that, if he was bent on unburdening his soul, he might build a monastery.

VESPASIANO DA BISTICCI

The Medici are very closely associated with the Convent of San Marco and

Every evening the monks of San Marco sing the Ave Verum in front of Fra Angelico's fresco of the Annunciation.

it has become the preferred meeting place for humanists and Neo-Platonists. The Dominican monks owe a great debt to Cosimo, who paid for the whole complex, including a colonnaded library by Michelozzo – the first in Europe to be open to the public. The gentle Fra Angelico lived here for many years, and decorated the cells of his fellow monks with representations of the life of Christ, witnessed by St Dominic. Fra Angelico was reputed to have been so deeply religious that he wept with emotion whenever he painted a crucifix. Cosimo reserved a cell in the convent for his visits, though it is rather grander than those of the monks.

More recently, however, there has been an upset to the close relationship between the Medici and San Marco. The Bolognese friar Girolamo Savonarola is a fierce critic of Florence's lax morality, blaming in particular Lorenzo, who is powerless to prevent the crowds flocking to hear Savonarola's sermons. The friar predicts that unless Florentines mend their ways disaster will strike.

SANTA CROCE AND THE PAZZI CHAPEL

Italy is the most intelligent country in Europe, Tuscany the most intelligent region of Italy, and Florence the most intelligent town in Tuscany.

THE BEGINNING OF A SERMON BY THE
FRANCISCAN ST BERNARDINO OF SIENA

The Franciscan church of Santa Croce faces the second largest piazza in Florence, where tournaments are held and popular Franciscan preachers deliver sermons. Since the Franciscans have inherited from their rivals the Dominicans the mantle as officers of the Inquisition, people also flock to the square to watch the burning of heretics. St Francis, founder of the order and an ardent advocate of the vow of poverty, would be amazed at the size of the church that Arnolfo di Cambio built here in around 1300; it is reputed to be as large as St Peter's in Rome.

The interior contains a number of splendid monuments to various important Florentine politicians and humanists, adorned with sculpture by Donatello and his followers. Two splendid classical-style tombs of chancellors of the Florentine Republic from earlier this century, Leonardo Bruni and Carlo Marsuppini, can be found on opposite sides of the nave. Both came from Arezzo – something that must have impressed Cosimo de' Medici, since he sent his son and heir Piero to be educated in that city, to the chagrin of top schoolmasters in Florence.

As soon as the church was built, rich Florentines flocked to acquire chapels. It is strange, however, how often ill fortune has beset these patrons. Giotto had scarcely finished painting chapels for the Peruzzi and Bardi, two of the richest banking dynasties in Florence, when both banks went spectacularly

Above *Although the Pazzi are personae non gratae in Florence, their memory lives on in Brunelleschi's exquisite Pazzi Chapel.*

Left *The monument to Leonardo Bruni in Santa Croce portrays the Florentine chancellor as a Roman senator.*

bankrupt, brought down in large part by the English king Edward III reneging on his debts (beating the French in a war lasting a hundred years was a very expensive business).

Similar ill fortune afflicted the Pazzi, whose exquisite chapel adjoining the church, designed by Brunelleschi, had just been completed when the family failed in their attempt to overthrow the Medici. You can admire the elegant pair of dolphins on the Pazzi coat-of-arms (this is just about the only place in Florence where you will still find it).

PONTE VECCHIO

The Ponte Vecchio is without doubt one of the great sights of Florence. The equestrian statue of Mars at the north end of the bridge marks the spot where Buondelmonte dei Boundelmonti was assassinated on Easter Day, 1216, beginning a war between Guelphs and Ghibellines that eventually consumed the whole of Tuscany. At the far end there stands a hospital of the Holy Sepulchre. This is the narrowest point on the river, where the current is strongest. Watch out if there is the possibility a flood. On more than one occasion, notably in 1333, the bridge has been swept away, drowning hundreds of Florentines.

There are some fifty businesses operating on the bridge, and you will find every sort of activity on offer: you can exchange money at the moneychangers, buy a pair of shoes at the cobblers, have your hair cut at the barbers, or even have your horse shoed by the blacksmiths. But don't take too much money with you, since this is a favourite haunt of pickpockets. In places the smell is pretty indescribable. The stalls of the fishmongers and tanners are bad enough, but pale in comparison with the leatherworkers who ply their trade by dipping the hides in the Arno, soaked in horse's urine. Halfway along the bridge watch out for a gap between the houses; this is where the butchers tip offal and waste into the river (don't watch this if you intend to dine on local fish).

BRANCACCI CHAPEL, SANTO SPIRITO AND PALAZZO PITTI

This Buonarotti and I from boyhood used to go to study in Masaccio's chapel in the Church of the Carmine; and because Buonarotti was accustomed to make fun of all those who were drawing there, one day when the said youth was annoying me among the rest, he aroused in me more anger than usual, and clenching my fist I gave him so violent a blow upon the nose, that I felt the bone and the cartilage break under the stroke, as if it had been a wafer; and thus marked by me he will remain as long as he lives.

PIETRO TORRIGIANI DESCRIBING THE FIGHT TO THE SCULPTOR BENVENUTO CELLINI

Young Michelangelo has been making a reputation for himself as the most promising artist in Florence but he has also been getting into trouble. Try asking the sacristans of Santa Maria del Carmine and Santo Spirito across the Arno. The one at the Carmine may well tell you that Michelangelo comes regularly to make drawings of the frescoes by Masaccio, whom he rates higher than any other painter, in the Brancacci Chapel. And if you give him a decent tip he will probably reveal the story of the violent fight between Michelangelo and his fellow artist Pietro Torrigiani. Torrigiani has since left Florence to avoid any recriminations.

The sacristan at Santo Spirito will probably be less willing to talk about Michelangelo, preferring instead to hold forth on the beauty of Brunelleschi's architecture (this is the last church he built). You may need to dig deeper into your purse before he will tell you that Michelangelo has offered to sculpt a crucifix for the Augustinian monks but, in exchange, he wants permission to cut up corpses in the convent's hospital so that he can make anatomical studies of them – a practice that is strictly forbidden.

If you find this all rather macabre, you can raise your spirits by looking at Palazzo Pitti nearby, which is one of the most splendid buildings in Florence. Luca Pitti, determined to outdo the Medici, was delighted to use the design by Brunelleschi that Cosimo had rejected for Palazzo Medici. It was rather typical of Pitti to have boasted that he had a palace built by the great Brunelleschi when work did not actually begin until twelve years after the architect's death.

Michelangelo's reverence for Masaccio is obvious from his drawn copy of St Peter from the Tribute Money *in the Brancacci Chapel.*

VI · GUILDS, TRADE AND TAX

THE GUILDS

A Florentine who is not a merchant, who has not travelled through the world, seeing foreign nations and peoples and then returned to Florence with some wealth, is a man who enjoys no esteem whatsoever.

GREGORIO DATI

Walking around the streets of Florence, admiring the splendour of the buildings, the lavish display in the shops and markets, and how well-dressed everyone seems to be, you may well wonder where this wealth comes from. The answer is banking and trade – especially of woollen cloth and silk.

Traditionally trade has been regulated by a guild system and this has been the main driving force of the Florentine economy for the past two centuries. There are seven major guilds and fourteen minor ones, and if you ask a prosperous merchant, he will swiftly tell you which one he belongs to. Whether he is a member of the cloth manufacturers (*Arte della Calimala*) or their rivals the wool-weavers (*Arte della Lana*), he will assure you that they are the oldest and most prestigious guilds, and that it was largely due to the enterprise of their members

that Florence became such a strong economic power in the last century. Warming to his theme, the merchant may continue by describing how the wool-weavers and cloth manufacturers made so much money that a separate guild was set up by the men who handled their financial affairs, the guild of money-changers, or as they prefer to be called, bankers (*Arte del Cambio*).

Florentines being such an argumentative people, you will not be surprised to find the influential judges and notaries among the senior guilds. They are a pompous lot and if you have any dealings with them, make sure you use their title of *messer*, and address them as *voi* rather than the more informal *tu*. The other members at the top table are the silk-weavers and the goldsmiths (both highly profitable trades), the doctors and apothecaries, and the furriers – furs being the most highly prized of all articles of clothing.

Members of these guilds are highly enterprising and industrious. Take the cloth merchants, who not only handle every aspect of the cloth trade but also make money in all sorts of other ways – for example, dealing in the import of spices, scents and expensive fabrics, and the export of wheat. They

A highly successful Florentine merchant (judging from the quality of his clothes) holds a letter, perhaps a bill of exchange.

poet Dante, who was of noble birth, as a member of their guild, which he chose for the social status it conferred. His contemporary, Giotto, had a more practical attitude, joining the same guild as a means to acquire pigments for his paintings.

The minor guilds (who are resentful of their inferior status) cover a multitude of professions ranging from linen drapers to stone-masons, carpenters, blacksmiths, salt, cheese and oil merchants, butchers, wine merchants, innkeepers, tanners, armourers, locksmiths and used-cloth dealers. Right at the bottom of the pile are the bakers, widely despised by the others because their profession is regarded as open to all comers. Regardless of which guild they join, however, there is one crucial criterion: members must be employers, not employees.

are very proud that the steel-tipped measuring stick they use is taken as a legal unit (called the *ell*) and forms the basis for all other units of length. The goldsmiths are equally versatile and creative, their members having a wide range of skills from cutting gemstones and designing gold plate to decorating furniture and chimney pieces. If you meet an artist, the chances are that he is a member of this guild; past and present members include Brunelleschi, Donatello, Ghiberti, Gozzoli, Uccello, Pollaiuolo and Verrocchio, to name but a few.

Each individual guild has its own hierarchical structure. Within the doctors and apothecaries' guild, for example, skilled physicians are ranked higher than apothecaries, with artists below them and grocers, barbers and haberdashers (who also sell drugs) lower still. They like to cite the great

The Agnus Dei, emblem of the guild of wool weavers (Arte della Lana), appears all over the city.

Regardless of their place in the pecking order, all the guilds are inordinately proud of their status. You will notice their emblems and coats-of-arms prominently displayed on buildings all over the city and will soon learn which guild each represents: the Agnus Dei for the wool weavers, the Virgin and Child for the doctors (St Luke, believed to have been a friend of the Virgin, was a doctor; he was also

Above Orsanmichele, decorated with some of the best sculptures in Florence, is next to the headquarters of the guilds.

Below Carving a masterpiece is a complicated business – look at all the implements in this relief showing the Art of Sculpture.

supposed to have painted the Virgin's portrait), gold coins for the money-changers. These emblems are an excellent way for the guild to show its munificence. The striking green-and-white marble façade of the church of San Miniato stands high on a hillside overlooking the Oltrarno. It was paid for by the cloth manufacturers. Never one to miss an opportunity to advertise its generosity, the guild inserted its emblem of an eagle holding a bale of cloth right at the centre of the façade.

If you have some business with one of the major guilds, you need to head for the area around Orsanmichele where they have their headquarters. You can tell how much money these guilds make from the numerous administrators, consuls, councillors, treasurers and accountants bustling about. The guilds take good care of their employees, providing pensions for the old and invalid, allowing the sick to take time off to visit medicinal baths, and even helping the needy to purchase clothes for their families. Charitable works often extend beyond the organization, too, with

several guilds patronizing a particular hospital and erecting splendid
buildings, both secular and ecclesiastical. Members of the silk guild are
very proud of the Foundling Hospital
Brunelleschi built for them earlier this
century, while there is a legendary
rivalry between the wool-weavers,
in charge of works at the Cathedral,
and the cloth manufacturers at the
Baptistery.

All this ostentation may hide the fact,
however, that in recent years the guilds
have been losing their power, and they
no longer have total control over their
workers' wages and working condi-
tions, including the power to discipline
them. As a result, you are unlikely to
see a bankrupt member suffering the
ritual humiliation at the New Market
where his bottom is struck three times
in front of the pillory.

*Here we see some of the stages in the
manufacture of woollen cloth, the basis
of Florence's wealth.*

THE WOOLLEN CLOTH
INDUSTRY

*A gentleman can be made with two
yards of red cloth.*

COSIMO DE' MEDICI

What you wear matters in Florence.
You can tell how seriously Florentines take clothing from the fact that
four of the seven major guilds are
devoted to aspects of the trade. Any
family that can afford it orders a new
set of garments every year. If you
want good-quality products and find
yourself arguing with a merchant over

the exorbitant cost of a jacket, just
remember how much effort has gone
into making the garment. There are
as many as twenty-seven individual
stages in the manufacture of a piece of
top-quality cloth.

Many stages in the process, including the washing, fulling (scouring
and beating) and dyeing of the cloth,
involve water, hence the vital importance of the city's position on the
river Arno. One of the great sights of
Florence is to go on a sunny morning
and watch the great timbers from the
forests of the Casentino being landed
from boats at the Piazza delle Travi
near Santa Croce. They are used for

This well-dressed wool merchant holds a pair of shears but looks as though he has never gone near a sheep in his life.

the beams (*travi*) of the dyers' drying-sheds. Nearby are the mills, and the barn-like sheds with hundreds of racks where the wool is hung out to dry.

All ranks of society help with the process, even monks. Members of the Benedictine order from the Ognissanti church rinse the wool in the river before laying it out on racks of woven reed. Unsurprisingly, they do not get involved in the first stage, when the wool is sorted and then washed in a mixture of horse urine and detergent. The workers who carry out this less appealing chore are famously rowdy and foul-mouthed.

The later stages, once the fullers have beaten the wool to remove any final impurities, are intricate and time-consuming. First it is combed, each handful receiving ten strokes, and the long and short filaments separated and carded. The yarn is now ready for spinning by women working at home. Lastly, independent masters dye the

BELLA FIGURA

Florentines believe that you can tell someone's status and even read their character, not only by his or her appearance but also by what he or she wears.

Every article of clothing – shirt, doublet, hose and gown for men, chemise, bodice and dress for women – is subject to intense analysis. Equally important is the material: linen or hemp for the lower orders, woollen cloth for daily wear. If you want to make a mark, you need to be seen wearing velvet, brocade or woven silk – or, even more extravagantly, embroidery embellished with fur trimmings.

You can scarcely believe the variety of fur on display: squirrel, rabbit and dormouse are the most common, but you will also see people wearing wolf and hare or, in winter, the thicker fur of marten, fox and polecat.

The most expensive and exotic furs are ermine, lynx and sable, which are normally saved for trimmings. A good salesman will tell you that a fringe of fur on the collar or cuffs accentuates the colour of the fabric. They will probably omit to inform you, however, that it is also a gathering place for bugs.

wool, an expensive process using alum to make fast the colours. Alum is much sought after and the Medici have taken control of the recently discovered mine at Tolfa, near Rome. The large profits from this mine were one of the causes of the bitter struggle between the Medici and the Pazzi.

At the head of whole enterprise is a highly competent manager, known as a *lanaiuolo*, of whom there are some 200 operating in Florence. Beneath him is the factor, who directs the daily operations of the shop, organizing and supervising the transformation of raw material, the fleeces imported from England or Spain, and the broker who delivers the wool, collects the yarn and pays the workers. To make sure the potential purchaser knows the quality of the item of clothing he or she is being offered, every piece of cloth is prepared and marked with a seal and label, rolled into a bale of felt or coarse linen, and doubled and stamped with the arms of the guild.

THE ART OF MERCHANT-BANKING

In the name of God and of profit.

MOTTO AT THE TOP OF COSIMO DE' MEDICI'S
BUSINESS LEDGER

Bankers are among the richest men in Florence. You will find them hard at work in the New Market. Any money-changer not operating here is ineligible for the guild. Despite their great success, or maybe because of it, these bankers are highly sensitive to the accusation that they are guilty of usury, of which the Catholic Church disapproves strongly. In theory the practice has been restricted to Jews or Jewish converts for the last half century and they are much hated for the extortionate rates of interest they charge (up to 30 per cent); however, everyone knows that the Medici and the other great banking families are every bit as bad. Just look at their magnificent palaces.

DYES

To run a successful business, it is vital to have the means to dye your clothes. The dyes themselves come from a variety of natural sources:

- Madder and realgar are used for red.
- Vermilion is the brightest red and comes from a crystalline substance on the shores of the Red Sea.
- Sulphurous acid is used for pearly white silk.
- Saffron yellow comes from fields of crocuses around San Gimignano.
- Purple-red comes from a lichen plant in Mallorca.
- Cochineal, a scarlet dye more commonly used to colour food, comes from crushing a small, Mediterranean beetle.
- Woad and indigo come from plants, and are used for shades of blue.
- Ultramarine, the most brilliant blue, comes from the expensive lapis lazuli stone.
- Some of the colours have nicknames: for example, brown is known as 'little monk', 'small beret' and 'lion's pelt'.
- The same dyes and pigments are mixed with either oil or egg to make the paints used by artists.

On the right a banker examines some florins while on the left his partner hands over a bill of exchange.

Before passing judgment on these merchant-bankers who appear to be earning a fortune so effortlessly, take a look at their background. It involves years of training, serving an apprenticeship abroad in the office of a merchant, usually as the factor or agent of a Florentine firm. The trainee banker can acquire fluency in at least one foreign language, as well as some knowledge of foreign weights, measures and tariffs, while learning how the market operates and forging useful contacts. There is a strong work ethic among businessmen in general. No wonder Giannozzo degli Alberti boasted that his ancestor Benedetto used to claim that 'he did so well in business [by] always having his hands stained with ink'.

What these merchant-bankers like is to diversify as much as possible, thus covering their risks. A cloth merchant invests in a shipment of spices and alum, while laying off the risk with his partners. Cautious merchants take out insurance, even on the lives of princes, as an untimely change of regime can be disastrous for business.

THE FLORIN

They are so beautiful that they give me great pleasure, because I love coins which are well designed; and you know that the more beautiful things are, the more they are cherished.

JACOPO PAZZI TO HIS FRIEND FILIPPO STROZZI

Fine things, and all bearing the stamp of our city. You can imagine how many we have, as it's we who coin them.

THE FLORENTINE AMBASSADOR REPLIES TO THE
DUKE OF MILAN WHEN SHOWN HIS TREASURE

The florin was first used in 1252 and soon became common currency all over Europe. It commemorated a theme that Florentines never tire of celebrating: defeating their local Tuscan rivals, in this case Pisa and Siena. It is a gold coin with an image of St John the Baptist, patron saint of the city, on one side, and a lily on other. By 1422 there were two million florins in circulation in both gold and silver. The process of making coins is quite simple. While the metal is soft it is placed on a flat surface and hit with a hammer with the stamp of the coin. This is done in the Mint (*Zecca*) next to the Palazzo della Signoria and then checked by goldsmiths for the purity of the metal and the quality of the workmanship although the silver-to-gold ratio constantly fluctuates. A florin is worth 7 lire, and a lira is worth 20 soldi or 60 quattrini.

Confusingly, there are several types of florin apart from the main *fiorino d'oro*: the *fiorino di suggello*, a sealed gold florin that has been weighed, tested and sealed in a purse in Florence; the *fiorino largo*, a large gold florin now worth 20 per cent more than the *fiorino di suggello*; the *fiorino largo di grossi*, the silver equivalent of the *fiorino largo*; and the *fiorino largo d'oro in oro*, a large gold coin that has only appeared recently, officially worth 19 per cent more than the *fiorino largo di grossi*. Just to add to the confusion, the florin is often called the *ducato*, most annoying for the Florentine government, as that is the name for the main Venetian currency. To give an example of the confusion, the Florentine merchant Francesco di Matteo Castellani borrowed some gold from

The florin incorporates two emblems of the city: the lily on one side, and St John the Baptist on the other.

his banker back in 1442. The loan consisted of three florins, and a number of ducats (three Venetian, three Roman, one Genoese and one Hungarian). No wonder the money-changers make so much money.

WAGES

You will not be surprised that top lawyers charge a fortune for their services, earning between 200 and 500 florins per annum. A leading university professor is on the same level. A bank manager earns rather less, between 100 and 200 florins per annum, much the same as a weaver in brocaded velvet, or the holder of a major church benefice. Treasury officials, average university professors, weavers in damask, accountants and successful tailors are on 100 florins per annum, while minor government officials, construction foremen and wool weavers are on 40–50 florins per annum. Carpenters and weavers of plain taffeta earn even less, with unskilled workers and pensioners at the bottom of the pile on less than 30 florins per annum. The cost of renting a house, meanwhile, is 25 florins per annum in central Florence, 10 florins per annum in the outskirts and half a florin for a slum.

A CHANGE IN THE MARKET

These days Florentines regard it as perfectly acceptable, even desirable,

BENCHMARKS

The use of a bench can tell you a lot about a nation's priorities.
Florentine merchants have a long bench outside their palaces. You will sometimes see a Florentine merchant discussing business, normally financial, with a client seated on one of these benches. The bench is so important that it gives its name – *banco* – to the business itself: the bank.

The ostentatiously wealthy Burgundians, much more concerned to spend money than to make it, spend so much of their time sitting on benches during their lavish feasts, that the feasts themselves are now named after them. They are called *banquettes*, or banquets.

If you have invested with a merchant and see the bench outside his palazzo is broken, or the table he does business on, head for the nearest bar and buy yourself a big drink, you will need it. It means his business is *banco rotto* (literally 'broken bench') – bankrupt.

to display their wealth since it is an expression of nobility and the source of their power and reputation. They call it *magnificentia*, and the greatest exponent, Lorenzo de' Medici, is called *il Magnifico*. This applies to clothes as much as to works of art or charitable donations. Silk-weavers produce more glamorous and expensive garments than the wool-weavers or cloth-manufacturers;

consequently, they are also much more profitable. The eighty or so silk-weavers' shops are filled with tempting arrays of splendid brocades, silken garments with paintings, spangles or filigree of gold. These are much sought after, not only in Florence itself but also throughout the princely courts of Italy, and beyond the Alps in France, the Low Countries and England.

The shopkeepers from whom you buy your clothes are free agents; they can buy and sell as they wish. The guilds no longer have the power to force them to do their bidding. The same applies to artists, who are increasingly regarded as figures in

This Florentine youth is busy reeling silk, one of the most profitable trades in Florence.

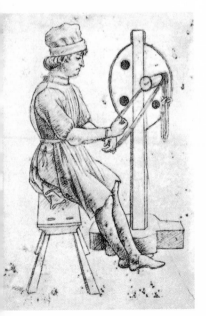

their own right and no longer mere craftsmen. Leonardo da Vinci epitomizes this change. Rulers from all over Europe are queuing up for his services and yet he seems to do exactly what he wants. And Lorenzo de' Medici is reputed to have so enjoyed the talent of young Michelangelo, who was studying in his sculpture garden, adjoining San Marco, that he allowed the aspiring sculptor to sit next to him at meals, above his son-in-law Franceschetto Cibo. Cibo, natural son of the Pope (and therefore a prince in his own right), regarded this as a serious slight to his dignity.

Although you will find shops crammed with highly desirable goods and the churches filled with beautiful works of art, many of the major businesses are in decline. In the wool and cloth trade, for example, there is strong competition from markets in the Netherlands. Even the Medici bank is struggling, and Lorenzo has been begging loans of cash from friends such as Filippo Strozzi whose fortune, in contrast, has grown enormously in recent years. Even worse, Lorenzo has succumbed to low practices: 'dipping' into the inheritance of his cousins Giovanni and Francesco, and raiding the *Monte dei Doti*, the government fund used to provide dowries for impoverished girls. This makes a strong contrast with his grandfather Cosimo, a banker first and foremost, who used his wealth judiciously.

TAX AND INVESTMENTS

We are in very poor condition, for we are paying heavy taxes and there is no trade on account of the plague.

FRANCESCO DATINI, MERCHANT OF PRATO,
FEBRUARY 1400

As Florentines spend so much time grumbling about how much tax they have to pay, it is as well to know something about the cause of their discontent. Their principal cause of complaint is the *Catasto* system of tax assessment, which assesses each citizen's possessions (real estate, business investments, communal bonds, cash and loans, plus debts and obligations) and the number in the household. This is levied twice a year, and three times in an emergency. There is a sliding scale with a highest rate of 22 per cent – meaning that some of the richest citizens have been paying tax at a punitive level of over 60 per cent some years. In 1473, Giovanni Rucellai paid the incredible sum of 60,000 florins in tax; not surprisingly, he went bankrupt just seven years later.

Florentines, of course, are racking their brains to think up ways to avoid paying tax. Cosimo de' Medici, for instance, kept a secret ledger especially for tax purposes that greatly overestimated losses due to bad debts. When questioned by officials, he merely replied: 'If there is an error in any item, either more or less, it is not malicious, or due to a wish to defraud,

THE MEDICI BANK

The Medici family bank was founded in 1397 by Giovanni di Bicci de' Medici. By his death he had amassed a fortune of 180,000 florins.

The bank was further expanded by his son Cosimo, who, though he professed a great love of civic democracy exercised rather rigid control over the business: there was certainly no board of directors. Such was Cosimo's wealth that he was reputed to have spent the fabulous sum of 600,000 gold florins in donations to charities and in various building projects, as well as in paying tax. At Lorenzo's succession in 1469, he inherited a fortune of over 230,000 florins.

There are branches of the Medici bank in Rome, Milan and Pisa, as well as in Geneva, Bruges, London, Avignon and Lyons. Each branch is a separate legal entity.

Goods handled by the bank include standard items such as wool, cloth, alum and olive oil, but also exotic spices and works of art.

but an error, which we are pleased to have recovered according to your discretion.' The officials, anxious not to offend the great man, accepted his word with alacrity and no more was said. A recent way of avoiding tax is to build new houses, which the government wishes to encourage; just last year it decreed that if you build on an empty site you are exempt from any tax for forty years – a strong inducement.

VII · RELIGION

A PART OF DAILY LIFE

When [Piovano] was with religious people, he argued about spiritual things; when he was with soldiers he reasoned with arguments suitable for them; when he was with merchants he reasoned in terms of commerce; when he was with women, gowned and well-bred, he conversed appropriately with some elegant, funny stories; and when he was with the bawdy women he had stories just for them.

A LATE 15TH-CENTURY COMMENTATOR ON
PIOVANO ARLOTTO, A COUNTRY PRIEST NOTED
FOR HIS RIBALD SERMONS

You will come across signs of the major role religion plays in Florentine life everywhere. It is rare to find a house without a devotional image, very often in the main bedroom, where it is a focus for meditation and prayer. Florentines attend church regularly, one of the few times you will see women outside the home. Morning mass and evening vespers are a standard part of daily routine – at least for people of a certain station – and workers are excused their labours on Saturday afternoons so that those in need of divine guidance can attend evening service. People from all classes give generously to beggars and in their wills make bequests to hospitals and convents, as well as making provision for masses to be recited for the souls of the departed. You cannot avoid the numerous religious processions around the city; the best place to view one is in the streets between the Cathedral and the Piazza della Signoria.

Sacred images are placed over doorways, and on street corners you will often see a crucifix or an image of the Virgin, surrounded by flowers or small gifts. They are regarded with veneration and just recently a man was hanged for stealing silver ornaments from a statue of the Virgin.

Fra Roberto Caracciolo preaches to a packed congregation – outwardly, at least, Florentines take their religion seriously.

The church of Santissima Annunziata has a miraculous image of the Annunciation, begun by a monk but finished by an angel (so it is believed), which is paraded through the streets during times of plague or famine. Florentines treat this image, and another from Santa Maria dell'Impruneta, with great reverence. If you want to add an offering to the hundreds of ex-votos that fill the chapel in Santissima Annunziata, given by grateful Florentines who have had their prayers answered, go to the Benintendi shop in via de' Servi, leading up to the church, which is filled with wax images.

Sacred relics are avidly collected and much venerated. There are always people entering the Baptistery to gaze at the relic of the True Cross given by the Emperor Charlemagne himself some 700 years ago. Only recently the guild of wool-weavers spent the fabulous sum of 800 florins commissioning a magnificent silver retable to house it, crafted by Antonio Pollaiuolo and Andrea Verrocchio.

The Medici paid for the chapel in Santissima Annunziata to house the image of the Annunciation and a charming chapel in the church of San Miniato by Michelozzo to house the crucifix that is said to have spoken to St John Gualberto, founder of the Vallombrosan Order of Tuscan monks based near Florence. To make sure everyone knows who paid for it, Piero de' Medici had the walls plastered with the ubiquitous Medici *palle*.

Florentines take pride in the city's leading religious figures. They remember with affection their great Archbishop Antonino Pierozzi, a friend of Cosimo de' Medici, who spent his life promoting peace in the city, founding schools for handicapped boys and girls, and hospitals for illegitimate children abandoned by their parents. He was a man of great humility and often appeared on foot or riding a mule. To show their respect and love for him, Florentines would kneel as he passed by. At his death his sole possessions were his mule and a few kitchen utensils.

St Bernardino of Siena commanded a similar devotion. He loved to preach to country folk and such was the power

St Bernardino addresses a vast crowd from the Palazzo Pubblico in his native Siena.

of his sermons that he could hold his audience for up to four hours, with stories interspersed with jokes. You can witness the power of contemporary preachers during Lent when an audience can be reduced to tears by accounts of the suffering of Christ and the lamentation of the Virgin.

Countrymen and women have a particular veneration for the Virgin, the traditional intercessor for sinners, the sick and the needy. Clutching their rosary or paternoster beads, you will come across them in wayside chapels reciting their Hail Maries. These peasants have responded ardently to the recent miraculous appearance of images of the Madonna on the wall of a prison in Prato and in a tannery in Cortona. As news spread, hundreds of pilgrims have flocked to the sites and two splendid churches have just been built to house those who come to worship.

FUNERARY CHAPELS

If I spend 2,000 florins on my house, my dwelling on earth, then 500 devoted to my residence in the next life seems to me money well spent.

PIERO DEL TOVAGLIA

When visiting the city's churches, you will notice the large number of privately owned chapels where families pay respect to their ancestors. The Church encourages the construction of these chapels; the cost of paying to have masses said for the dead provides a major source of income. These funerary chapels, often lavishly decorated with altarpieces and frescoes, demonstrate the piety of the donors but also their wealth and social position.

The churches belonging to the three main religious orders (the Franciscans, Dominicans and Augustinians) attract the most artistic patronage because they are perceived to give you the best chance of reaching heaven. Florentines believe passionately in purgatory and hell. Take the Strozzi chapel in Santa Maria Novella, which has a highly realistic fresco of the Last Judgment by Nardo di Cione – no detail has been spared in the depiction of hell, which is based on Dante's famous description in the *Inferno*. This so impressed the Pope of the day back in 1344 that he gave Strozzi a remission of 515 days in purgatory. Strozzi had no doubt that this would help his cause in the afterlife: he and his wife are depicted at the Last Judgment being led by an angel into paradise. If you happen to witness a mass in one of these chapels, you will find no expense spared in the ecclesiastical regalia on view: candlesticks, chalices, censers and missals.

THE CONFRATERNITIES

There are some seventy-five religious confraternities in Florence, companies of like-minded men devoted to cults of saints. They meet in the mornings and evenings to sing hymns, and on a Sunday you will often come across them processing to the Cathedral. These confraternities are dedicated to good works and charitable purposes; many of them run schools, while others help the lowest members of society. For example, the Company of Santa Maria del Bigallo, based opposite the Baptistery, take care of orphans in the Foundling Hospital (see p. 23). To honour the members' good work, the Company is allowed to select prisoners for release once a year. The Company of the Misericordia is also much respected. The members tend the sick and supervise the burial of the poor, though some wags maintain that the confraternity's building was originally financed with the proceeds of a swear box.

You will learn to recognize the various emblems the members wear on their robes: caps with angel-and-dove insignia for the Company of the Annunciation, yellow crosses on a red background for the Company of St Mary, a crucifix suspended under a martyr's crown for the Company of St Sebastian. The banners of the confra-

As we have to prepare for the Feast of the Magi, these things [simple dress] will make a change from my cloth of gold.

COSIMO DE' MEDICI'S WIFE
TO HER SON

ternities are equally ornate, many of them displaying the Virgin or Christ on the cross.

These confraternities are yet another example of the way in which Florentines of all social classes mix. The grandest patrician is quite happy to sit beside a lowly workman at the meetings of their particular confraternity. On Holy Thursday, the normal social order is reversed and the most senior members wash the feet of the brethren as well as offer them a simple meal, to commemorate Christ washing the feet of his disciples. The brothers will then sing hymns together before sharing a meal.

Lorenzo de' Medici is a member of seven confraternities in total and takes his duties very seriously. He is President of the Confraternity of the Magi that meets every Tuesday in the Sacristy of San Marco. Lorenzo consciously attempts to emulate his grandfather Cosimo who used to give his fellow brothers gifts of flour, eggs and wine, as well as offering to help them with arranging their daughters' dowries.

Some of these confraternities maintain close connections with the countryside. If you are up at dawn, you may hear their members leaving the city, singing praises to Christ and the Virgin as they make their way to the fields owned by the confraternity where they will spend the day working.

the soil and tending the vines. In the evening they return home, bearing agricultural produce. After harvest they sell grain in the market. They also hire labourers to fertilize the fields with night soil taken from stables and town houses.

THE FLAGELLANTS

The Company of Jesus wear white sack-cloth with a vermilion crucifix on the left shoulder, belted with a cord of hemp. And when they go outside they go bare-footed with their faces hidden, striking themselves with whips of white leather. Within the meeting hall they whip themselves with rope whips in order to dampen the noise and sound.

A CONTEMPORARY CHRONICLE

Many Florentine men are deeply affected by the memory of Christ's suffering and have joined together in confraternities devoted to penitential practices. Men from all ranks of society join these brotherhoods, which are known as *Disciplinati* (those who are whipped) from their practice of flagellating themselves, a way of purging their bodies of sin and thus purifying their souls. Lorenzo de' Medici is a member of the Confraternity of San Paolo, which specializes in distributing alms to the poor. There are strict rules: members must say daily prayers (between five and fifteen Hail Maries and Our Fathers), and fast one day a week. They celebrate all major feasts, mourn the dead, and pay their dues to the confraternity.

Though this was once a common sight, you will still sometimes see members of a confraternity parading through the streets on special feast days in their hooded white robes with hemp belts, carrying whips made of rope. Their garments are slit open at the back from shoulder to waist, but, since this is a city devoted to fashion, they 'wear the garment in such a manner that one is uncovered modestly, without appearing nude'. These acts of flagellation are also performed in private in the confraternity's oratory.

The behaviour of those who wish to join a confraternity is scrutinized by existing members to ensure that there is nothing that will taint the purity of the brotherhood. Members are required to make monthly confessions. Vices that cause shame or lead to violence are strictly forbidden: for example, drinking in taverns on the days of confraternal services, frequenting brothels, practising sodomy and playing games of chance for money. If a new member has committed usury (highly likely if he is a banker) he must go to the abbot to receive a penalty and make restitution to the injured party. Punishments can even include being ordered to go on a pilgrimage – most inconvenient if you are a successful businessman.

FLORENTINE AMBIVALENCE
TOWARDS RELIGION

*Not for the love of God, but because you
need it.*

DONATELLO, GIVING ALMS TO A BEGGAR

If it sounds as though the Florentines
are a deeply religious people, there is
also a feeling among many highly educated citizens that the Catholic Church
has grave failings, and you will notice
that anticlericalism is very pervasive.
The clergy is powerful and owns one
third of all the land in Tuscany, and
many people think that they abuse
their position, not least by indulging
in the practice of simony (the buying
and selling of benefices). In addition,
Florentines remember all too well that
it was two priests who very nearly succeeded in assassinating Lorenzo de'
Medici in 1478, after the hardened
mercenary leader Giovanni Battista de
Montesecco refused to commit such a
sacrilegious deed in church.

*Despite their ambivalence towards religion,
Florentines love beautiful works of art, as this
illuminated manuscript, owned by Lorenzo
de' Medici, demonstrates.*

This ambivalence towards religion
is particularly evident among the
circle surrounding Lorenzo. These
Neo-Platonists take religion seriously, but their search for forms of
knowledge outside Christianity has
drawn down the wrath of the Church;
indeed, the leading philosophers Marsilio Ficino and Pico della Mirandola
are suspected of heresy. And how the
Church longs to discipline Lorenzo's
close friend, the writer Luigi Pulci,
who has been heard joking that Moses

loosed the floodgates of a mere fish-
pond to drown a few of Pharaoh's men,
and that Samson may have carried off
the doors of a summer-house, not
the Temple. Even more scandalously
he has quipped that when St Peter
the first head of the Catholic Church
walked on water he was actually crossing a frozen sea. Pulci's jokes are in
keeping with Florentines who mock fat
monks overindulging in communion
wine and leering at attractive women
in the confessional.

IX (Previous page) *In the upper of these two scenes, money-changers are hard at work; one of them stashes his money away in a coffer.*

Below, a group of Florentines queue up to pay their taxes while a clerk enters their details in a ledger. Note the elaborate carpet on the table.

X (Above) *The full splendour of Benozzo Gozzoli's* Procession of the Magi *in the chapel of Palazzo Medici. The more observant will spot the (admittedly idealized) portraits of the young Lorenzo and his father Piero, 'the Gouty'.*

XI (Right) *Florentines go about their daily business in the Piazza della Signoria, paying scant interest to the burning of the fearsome preacher Savonarola in the centre of the square. Behind is the Palazzo della Signoria.*

XII (Opposite above) *A big crowd has assembled in Piazza Santo Spirito to watch a game of football, a highly popular Florentine pastime.*

XIII (Below) *Horsemen bear banners, known as* pali, *to the Baptistery on the feast day of St John the Baptist, patron saint of Florence. They are welcomed by Florentines decked out in their finest clothes.*

XIV *Ambrogio Lorenzetti's wonderfully vivid depiction of Siena shows the city enjoying peace and prosperity with workers plying their trades while a group of maidens dance in the street.*

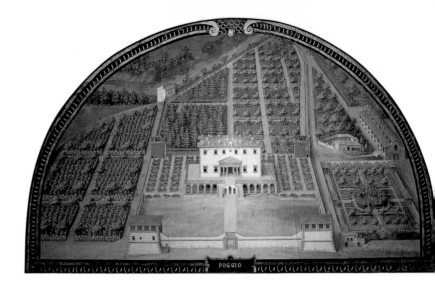

XV (Above) *A bird's eye view of Lorenzo de' Medici's favourite villa, at Poggio a Caiano. The illustration shows clearly the time and energy Lorenzo has spent on laying out the surroundings of the villa.*

XVI (Below) *The city of Siena appears as a forest of towers surrounding the gleaming white façade of the Cathedral. It rests in the hands of the Blessed Ambrogio Sansedoni, one of the city's patron saints.*

SCANDAL

They cheat, steal and fornicate, and when they are at the end of their resources, they set up as saints and work miracles, one displaying the cloak of St Vincent, another the handwriting of St Bernardino, a third the bridle of Capistrano's donkey.

MASUCCIO SALERNITANO ON THE
MINORITE ORDER

Many Florentines you will meet have sisters, aunts and nieces in the fifty convents in and around the city, which cater for some 2,000 nuns. Most are incarcerated for life, often against their will, because it is impossible to raise enough money for a suitable dowry. Entering Florence from the north you will pass ten convents on via San Gallo alone. With so many nuns unsuited to their vocation, whiling away endless hours embroidering clothes for their families, there are bound to be some who fail to honour the vow of chastity – which may be why so many convents are surrounded by high and seemingly impenetrable walls.

You have already heard about the libidinous activities of Fra Filippo Lippi (p. 67) who eloped with the beautiful nun Lucrezia Buti. This was not an isolated example, however. At the Augustinian convent of Santa Caterina de Cafaggiolo two nuns bore children back in the 1460s, something that profoundly shocked Archbishop Antonino. Senior religious figures are

no better behaved. Not long ago, at San Salvi, just outside the city walls, the abbot was discovered to have been smuggling his mistress into his cell at night. Even worse, Mariano, Abbot of Silva, took a peasant's wife as his mistress. When the cuckolded husband protested, the abbot tried to have him murdered. The church, of course, is anxious to emphasize that these stories are isolated examples and in no way typical, but it is on dangerous ground.

Look at the behaviour of the pope. Lorenzo de' Medici has recently made an extremely advantageous match by marrying his fifteen-year-old daughter Maddalena to Innocent VIII's 'nephew' Franceschetto Cibo. As everyone knows, this unattractive, boorish man, now forty years old and perpetually drunk, is, in fact, the pope's natural son. There are lots of jokes on the theme of nepotism, where 'everyone is allowed to call the pope "papa" except his own children'.

Lorenzo's famed diplomatic skills have been incredibly successful in his dealings with the papacy. Just a decade ago he was excommunicated in the wake of the Pazzi Conspiracy. Now, not only has his daughter married the pope's son, but, even more importantly, Lorenzo's son Giovanni has recently been elevated to the rank of cardinal at the tender age of thirteen for a reputed cost of 100,000 florins (money well spent if one day he becomes pope). Lorenzo is absolutely delighted, declaring it to be 'the great-est achievement of our house'.

With his father's 'assistance', Gio-vanni's career has been remarkably successful. He was created an abbot at the age of seven and now possesses twenty-seven benefices and a canonry in every cathedral in Tuscany. There have been terrific festivities to cele-brate Giovanni becoming a cardinal, something that Lorenzo is at pains to stress is to the great benefit of all Florence (though it is an even better way for Lorenzo to advance his fami-ly's interests). No wonder there is a constant stream of wagons trundling down the via Cassia heading for the Vatican, laden with the best Trebbiano wine, delicate Tuscan cheeses and the finest Florentine cloth – all gifts for the pope who accepts them grate-fully while insisting that elections to the College of Cardinals are totally impartial.

Wherever you go in Florence, you will find that Lorenzo is a major topic of conversation, not least for his puzz-ling decision to bring Savonarola back to the Convent of San Marco, osten-sibly at the instigation of Pico della Mirandola. Maybe Lorenzo has a trou-bled conscience, and wants to give this man of God a hearing – even though he knows perfectly well that Savon-arola is opposed to his championship of Neo-Platonism. Already the friar is making his mark, and showing his desire to reform not only the Church, but also Florentine society.

SAVONAROLA

A Dominican Friar has so terrified a the Florentines that they are wholly give up to piety.

AN ENVOY FROM MANTU

Here is a stranger come into my hous who will not even deign to visit me.

LORENZO DE' MEDICI ON SAVONAROLA ARRIVAL IN FLORENC

Girolamo Savonarola, originally fror Ferrara, is a terrifying looking char acter with his piercing grey eyes, thic red lips and hooked nose. He ha made a big impact since his recen arrival in the city but the friar ha refused to visit his patron, incitin Lorenzo's displeasure. Forswearing a

This stark portrait amply reflects Savonarola's austere character.

There is no mistaking the grip of Savonarola's oratory as he holds his audience spellbound from the pulpit.

comfort, he stalks the streets dressed in a coarse black robe. Fra Girolamo's sermons delivered in San Marco during Lent in a harsh voice, accompanied by violent gestures, have been electrifying Florentines and you will be lucky to gain admittance through the crowds who throng to hear his powerful preaching. Some of his audience record that his words have the effect of thunderclap, with a cold shiver running visibly through the ranks of listeners.

If Florentines heed his advice that anyone who consorts with prostitutes or sodomites, or reads the pagan works of Aristotle and Plato, or collects wanton images of pagan subjects is guilty of sin, then there are few who can hold up their heads without shame. For those who persist in their dissolute ways, the horrors of hell await – which Savonarola describes in detail. Furthermore, the friar is urging

his listeners not only to repent themselves, but also to reform others so that society can be cleansed. The ruling class, whom he accuses of corruption

A FIERY END

Following Lorenzo's death in 1492, and the French invasion of Italy two years later, the Medici will be expelled from Florence and Savonarola will take over the government and instigate an austere theocracy. In 1497 his Bonfire of the Vanities in the Piazza della Signoria will consume priceless works of art including paintings by Botticelli. A year later the Florentines, tired of this era of austerity, and the fact that the corrupt Borgia Pope Alexander VI has excommunicated him, will turn on Savonarola, who is tortured and burnt at the stake in the very same piazza on 28 May 1498.

and lax morality, are understandably nervous. His powerful words have, however, produced a new atmosphere in the city. Fra Girolamo is tipped to be the next Prior of San Marco.

SUPERSTITION AND SORCERY

Astrology is a vice that the Florentines have inherited from their idolatrous Roman ancestors.

MATTEO VILLANI

Florentines are intensely superstitious, forever worrying about ill fortune. They regard Saturday as a day of bad luck and are reluctant to embark on a journey on that day. Every family of consequence consults an astrologer who casts children's horoscopes. Lorenzo's friend, the philosopher Marsilio Ficino, is reputed to have predicted that his second son, Giovanni, will become pope. Women who desire to have children employ a variety of talismans, amulets and herbal remedies to attract good fortune. Even the poorest urchin wears a talisman. One was found recently wearing a priceless antique gem round his neck. It is now one of the most prized pieces in Lorenzo's collection.

Florentines are also fascinated by magic. Cosimo Rosselli, who has recently been painting the walls of the Sistine Chapel in Rome alongside Botticelli and Ghirlandaio, is keen on alchemy, and hopes to find the elusive secret that will transform base metal into gold. Lorenzo, like most of his fellow citizens, believes in palmistry and you will often observe Florentines having their palms read. They believe that a long hand with a broad palm is a warning that the person is mischievous, even a knave or a thief, whereas if a woman has a short hand with excessively long fingers, she will be in peril during childbirth.

There are others who have a darker view of magic. Fiesole, rising up the hillside just to the north of Florence, is reputed to be a centre of sorcery and witchcraft. There are tales of strange beings coming to draw water at the well in the village, creatures with false eyes that they remove and put back as old men do with their teeth. The religious authorities take a very tough line with anyone suspected of witchcraft. In his papal bull of 1484, Innocent VIII authorized that, after a trial (usually cursory), the witch should be burnt in public.

VIII · FESTIVALS AND TOURNAMENTS

CARNIVAL

We also have some beanpods, long
And tender morsels for a pig.
We have still others of this kind,
But they're well cooked, quite firm,
    and big,
And each will make a foolish clown
If you first take the tail in hand
Then rub it gently up and down.

LORENZO DE' MEDICI, *RIBALD SONG OF THE*
VILLAGE LASSES

Be careful as you beat that you don't beat
so hard that the batter splashes out.
When it is finished, taste it with your
finger and if it seems ready, place the
irons in the fire.

FROM *CANTI CARNAVALESCHI*, A SERIES OF
RIBALD LYRICS, SOME BY LORENZO DE' MEDICI

You should try to ensure that your visit coincides with a major Florentine festival, a wonderful mixture of theatre, religious spectacle and sport. They range from the restrained welcome given to visiting foreign dignitaries, to the joyful celebration of May Day and the feast of St John. The most exuberant by far is Carnival, during which all the main streets of the city are inundated with banners, gilded coats-of-arms and rich tapestry hangings draped from palace windows overlooking the vast and boisterous crowds.

You can don your mask and join the daily parades through the streets. Women are, in theory, banned from the processions, but there is every opportunity to flirt with attractive girls who are watching from windows and balconies. When carousers began

Florentine ladies at their windows are
serenaded by a group of singers during
Carnival.

throwing snowballs at the window of Marietta Strozzi, as Lorenzo de' Medici was told, one 'succeeded in flinging snow upon the maiden's face', but the feisty Marietta retaliated, 'so graceful, so skilled in the game, and beautiful, as everyone knows, and acquitted herself with great honour'.

During Carnival the floats of the various guilds and confraternities are filled with allegorical and mythological characters, accompanied by a motley array of figures dressed as satyrs, nymphs, clowns, beggars, hermits, astrologers and devils, all chanting obscene songs. The crowds cheer licentious Eros, the mischievous god of love who is blindfolded and wears multicoloured wings, and Bacchus, the inebriated god of wine who seems about to tumble off his float. After dark, revellers process through the streets brandishing torches and fireworks illuminate the night sky. One year the maverick, reclusive painter Piero di Cosimo designed a float depicting the Triumph of Death. Covered in black cloth with skeletons and white crosses painted on, it was drawn by black buffaloes; on top stood a figure of Death, holding a scythe and surrounded by tombs.

More usually, crowds of happy Florentines can be seen marching through the streets, banging their drums and singing the scandalous songs that Lorenzo composes for Carnival. He is particularly popular among the lower classes who feel free to take liberties during the general mayhem, referring to themselves ironically as baronies or principalities (*potenze*), and their leaders calling themselves kings or emperors. You can recognize them from the great flags they wave, emblazoned with their emblem.

THE FEAST OF ST JOHN THE BAPTIST

As you make your way along the streets, the houses are all hung with tapestries and the chairs and benches covered with taffeta. Everywhere you see girls and young women dressed in silk and bedezined with jewels, precious stones and pearls.

A 15TH-CENTURY VISITOR TO FLORENCE

In the morning all the Guilds have displays outside their shops of all their rich things, ornaments and jewelry. They display enough gold and silk to adorn ten kingdoms...

GREGORIO DATI ON THE EVE OF THE FESTIVAL

On 23 June, the day before the feast of Florence's patron, St John the Baptist, shopkeepers decorate their shops with cloth of gold. At midday the clergy lead a procession, singing songs and bearing sacred relics. Some of them are dressed as saints and angels, often causing irreverent jocularity among the onlookers. In the evening, members of the Signoria lead an even larger procession consisting of civic worthies representing the sixteen quarters of the city, senior clergymen, members of the confraternities and guilds, and envoys from the subject towns of Tuscany. They march to the Baptistery where they offer tributes of painted wax mounted on great wooden structures.

On the feast day itself, make sure you go to Piazza della Signoria where you will be greeted with a magnificent spectacle: one hundred gilded and revolving towers, representing the subject towns, covered with depictions of horsemen, soldiers, dancing girls and animals. Representatives of these 'cities' pay a token tribute, as do feudal lords who owe allegiance to the commune and delegates from rural parishes. More processions make their way to the Baptistery where the piazza is covered with blue tents adorned with yellow lilies. Last year the festival of St John the Baptist was even more splendid than usual, as Lorenzo chose this auspicious day for the wedding of his daughter Maddalena to Franceschetto Cibo.

The processions are followed by a midday feast with a display of dishes: roast meats, boiled capons in spiced gravy, trout, fresh pasta, saffron puddings and egg custards with burnt sugar coating. Afterwards, there are all sorts of entertainments to watch. The most popular is the Palio, a highly competitive horse race and a cause of much betting. The race runs from the Porta al Prato to Porta Santa Croce

A procession of Florentine notables makes its way with due solemnity into the Baptistery on the feast of St John.

through the streets in the centre of the city, with packed crowds of cheering spectators within touching distance of the galloping horses.

Equally exciting is the Calcio, a violent game of football played by young Florentine working-class men. It is a game of two teams of twenty-seven players each, chosen from different quarters of the city. This is local rivalry at its fiercest. Don't worry too much about the rules, much of the game seems to be devoted to beating the opposition into submission, regardless of where the ball is. Watch out if you are invited to join in, you could do yourself a serious injury.

OTHER FESTIVALS

The Florentine calendar boasts some ninety-three feast days, of which forty are public holidays. The majority of these feasts are religious in origin, and are one of the few times when almost everybody attends mass. Locals, rich and poor alike, love to celebrate these feast days with parades: for example, members of the Foundling Hospital carry a panel of the Madonna of Charity, holding open her cloak to protect foundlings, who are depicted in swaddling clothes or brown smocks, their hands clasped in prayer.

Religious fervour is at its most intense between Christmas and Epiphany, and during Lent. This latter period is a time for reflection and abstinence, and the Cathedral is packed with thousands who come to hear sermons by famous preachers hired by the commune. On Palm Sunday, the clergy process from the Baptistery across the piazza to the Cathedral, bearing olive sprigs that are then distributed to the people.

On Easter Saturday stones brought back from Christ's tomb in the Holy Land are used to relight the lamps that were extinguished on Good Friday. Until 1478 this was the prerogative of the Pazzi family, whose ancestor Pazzo de' Pazzi, the first to plant his flag on the walls of Jerusalem during the First Crusade, had brought back the stones. But since the family's attempt to overthrow the Medici, the Pazzi name has been obliterated from the city's records.

As well as the major regional holidays, you may also like to witness one of the numerous local feasts, often celebrating an individual saint, which possess a charm of their own. They most often consist of a religious cere-

mony followed by a feast during which vast quantities of food and wine are consumed. This is how the dyers celebrate the feast of St Onofrio on 11 June, ending with a horse race down Corso dei Tintori, the street named after their trade.

Florentines are very fond of the feast of the Annunciation on 25 March, which heralds the Tuscan spring. Many of their best artists, including Leonardo, Donatello and Fra Angelico, have depicted the event in paintings and sculpture. If you are in the city on that day, go to the church of Santa Maria del Carmine on

Florentine maidens present gifts to Lorenzo during May Day festivities – note the Medici palle *on the street corner.*

In this cassone Florentines have turned out to welcome Emperor Frederick III to the Piazza del Duomo on his visit in 1452.

the Oltrarno (a typical working-class neighbourhood), and you will find that the Carmelite order fill the church with flowers, particularly lilies, which are associated with the Madonna.

May Day is another popular festival when girls, wearing their prettiest spring frocks and carrying leafy branches, dance in Piazza Santa Trinita, while young men hang sprigs of May blossom, adorned with ribbons, on the doors of their homes. Lorenzo, always keen to court popularity, only last year wooed the lowly wool-workers of the Oltrarno (traditionally an anti-Medici area) during their May Day celebrations by lending their leader, the self-styled 'King of Camaldoli', cups, bowls and goblets for a feast.

At the church of Santa Trinita, in a more prosperous area across the Arno, the Valombrosan order celebrates 31 May, the feast of the Trinity, by providing an outdoor banquet for the entire neighbourhood with whole oxen roasted on a spit and then consumed with eggs, bread, salad, fruit and quantities of good Tuscan wine. Musicians and singers entertain the crowd, and perhaps you will see 'a Catalan named Bartalotto who performed many fine tumbling acts and feats of strength and other marvellous things', who appeared one year.

Leading families believe that it will help their ancestors in the afterlife if they are commemorated in feasts associated with key religious figures. Lorenzo de' Medici celebrates the feast day of his namesake in the Medici parish church of San Lorenzo, where his ancestors are buried. He has also chosen to commemorate his murdered brother Giuliano on the feast of St Stephen, the day after his birthday, and his mother Lucrezia on the day of the Visitation of the Virgin.

Music plays an important part in these festivals, particularly during the spring. Wherever you walk in the city, you will come across bands of drummers and trumpeters, and street musicians singing ballads of love, madrigals and local favourites called *rispetti* and *strambotti*. Rich and poor alike sing together several times a week in the Piazza San Martino, where the confraternity of Good Men (Buonomini) of San Martino helps those too ashamed to beg.

The famous Flemish composer Heinrich Isaac, organist at the Cathedral, can often be seen making his way to Palazzo Medici where he is teaching Lorenzo's children music. They will learn some of the new instruments that have become fashionable: harpsichords, organs, viols, lutes, harps and horns. Florentines love to dance. Their favourites are the *Pavane*, a solemn stately dance, the *Galliard*, an exuberant dance in triple time, and the *Alemande*, another lively dance of German origin, accompanied by the lute.

PLAYS

It is well worth going to see the sacred plays that are held in churches and open piazzas. Performances are normally held in the evening, between vespers and nightfall. The Confraternity of the Magi's annual play at Epiphany is the most splendid in Florence – unsurprisingly, considering that Lorenzo is the society's head.

Plays, in general, are of a very high standard. On the feast of the Ascension, the church of the Carmine is filled with flowers and banners hung from the walls. In the middle of the nave stands a stage with figures representing God the Father and Christ suspended from beams, with children dressed as angels in the clouds alongside. When the performance begins, Christ descends to the stage, acts his part before being pulled up again into the clouds, while the angels scatter rose petals. No wonder Lorenzo's son Giovanni has been so keen to take a leading part in a performance of the *Representation of St John and St Paul* written by his father. Music plays a major part in these plays. People still remember the brilliance and drama of Poliziano's *Orfeo*, a highly original piece with actors singing the lines.

JOUSTS AND TOURNAMENTS

In these peaceful times, [Lorenzo] kept his fatherland always in festivities; there frequent jousts and representations of old deeds and triumphs were to be seen; and his aim was to keep the city in abundance, the people united, and the nobility honoured.

NICCOLÒ MACHIAVELLI

The wonderful pageantry that attends Florentine tournaments is a golden opportunity for the city's leading families to put on a public display of their wealth and power. Tournaments are normally held in the large open space of Piazza Santa Croce. The piazza itself is covered in sand and divided with wooden rails to allow the jousting horsemen to ride full tilt at one another. The surrounding buildings are hung with an array of banners and pennants, with the city's dignitaries eated in tiers of seats in front of the basilica. It is a glorious sight and not to be missed when the riders canter into the piazza, their armour covered in silk and velvet, and their family emblems picked out in gold and silver thread. Even the horses' saddles and coats are covered in jewels.

Florentines still remember the tournament in honour of Lorenzo in 1469, a true display of princely magnificence. He appeared dressed in a red and white surcoat and a jewel-encrusted black velvet cap. His standard was painted specially by Verrocchio for the occasion, with a portrait of Lorenzo's mistress, Lucrezia Donati, weaving a laurel-wreath (a pun on Lorenzo's name) in the centre. His mistress Lucrezia herself presented him with the prize of a silver helmet. Seven years later the Medici staged another magnificent tournament in honour of Lorenzo's brother Giuliano, who wore silver armour designed by Verrocchio and carried a standard painted by Botticelli with his mistress Simonetta Vespucci in the guise of Pallas-Athene.

Several of the larger piazzas stage mock jousts. The Joust of the Saracen (*Giostra del Saracino*) is one of the most enjoyable. An armoured knight with levelled lance gallops at the target of a Moor, aiming either for his head or his heart. If he misses he may well end up on his backside on the earth. There is another spectacular joust every year to commemorate Florence's conquest

This painting captures all the pageantry of a tournament in Piazza Santa Croce. Every window is packed with spectators.

of Pisa. The young gallants, wearing their family colours and riding richly caparisoned horses, love this opportunity to display their martial prowess. To show their ardour, on the way to the joust they strike their lance against the side of the house of their beloved.

There is, however, a sense of unreality to these splendid, chivalric events. A year after his tournament, Lucrezia was forgotten and Lorenzo had made a dynastic marriage to Clarice Orsini, a member of the aristocratic Roman family. His fellow citizens crowded into the Palazzo Medici to enjoy a series of banquets over three days, the guests devouring hundreds of calves and 2,000 brace of capons, washed down by 100 barrels of wine, while fifty girls danced at the bride's table.

EXECUTIONS

And because the people of Santa Maria Nuova saw that he was still unrepentant and still talked of some vendettas and the like, the Magistrates decided to hang him again, and so he was.

A DIARIST OF 1487 RECORDING HOW A
CRIMINAL WAS CUT DOWN BEFORE HE WAS
DEAD, KEPT IN HOSPITAL FOR TWO WEEKS,
AND THEN HANGED AGAIN

If an execution is to take place during your stay in Florence, you will very likely hear a herald announce the event a few days beforehand. Executions take place outside the city and there is a set route passing Florence's principal monuments: the Podestà, the Cathedral, the Old Market (where the condemned kneel before the Tabernacolo della Tromba), the Piazza della Signoria and Santa Croce, before leaving the city by the Gate of Justice. Two streets are even named after these processions, via dei Malcontenti and via dei Neri – the latter getting its name from the Black Company (a section of the Confraternity of St Mary of the Cross at the Temple, of which Lorenzo de' Medici is a member), who escort the condemned man in a cart, as he makes his way to the gallows.

The darker side of the Florentine character comes to the fore as the crowd hurls abuse at the criminals, some of whom have already been tortured, usually by red-hot pincers. These same people enjoy the bizarre and macabre ceremony known as the Knight of the Cat that occasionally accompanies a wedding, where a shaven-headed man, stripped to the waist, is shut in a cage with an infuriated cat, which he has to kill with his teeth.

Sometimes the spectators sympathize with a condemned criminal, as occurred in April 1465, when they watched in shocked silence as a mere slip of a girl, barely twelve years old, sentenced for killing the infant daughter of the goldsmith Bernardo della Zecca, was taken to her death. It has even been known for the crowd to intervene. Once, in Piazza del Grano, convinced that there had been a miscarriage of justice, the crowd surged forward and released two prisoners 'with a great scream as if they had won all the world's treasures', as one bystander noted. Usually, however, no mishap occurs and the condemned man or woman is led to the place of execution where the Black Company have a cemetery and chapel where they can pray, hear mass and take communion before the hangman performs his grisly job.

IX · THE SURROUNDINGS
OF FLORENCE

Outside the city walls are beautiful dwellings of citizens with decorated gardens of wonderful beauty; and the countryside is so full of palaces and noble dwellings and so full of citizens that it seems to be a city.

GREGORIO DATI

This park is a source of great consolation, not only to ourselves and our neighbours, but also to strangers and travellers who pass by in the heat of summer...who can refresh themselves with clear and tasty water.... And no traveller does not stop for quarter of an hour to view the garden filled with beautiful plants.

GIOVANNI RUCELLAI ON HIS
PROPERTY AT QUARACCHI

Although Florentines live and work in the city, they have a deep love of the countryside. As soon as you leave the gates of the city, you will see hundreds of handsome villas dotting the surrounding cypress-clad hills. They are perfect places to escape from the heat of the city in summer. As close as Arcetri, a short walk up the hill on the south bank of the Arno, the Villa Gallina has some remarkable decoration, a delightful room frescoed with dancing nudes. On the north side of the city Francesco Sassetti, with all the money he has made at the Medici bank, has built a beautiful villa called La Pietra.

To the west of Florence, at Quaracchi, Giovanni Rucellai (the same responsible for the façade of Santa Maria Novella) built a wonderful villa. The family have always maintained good relations with their tenants, to whom they leased the land for several generations, and when Giovanni went bust a decade ago, the grateful peasants stepped in and have continued to maintain his garden at their own expense. And when his son Bernardo married Nannina de' Medici, the peasants gave the couple a magnificent olive tree in a cart.

FIESOLE

When you are made uncomfortable by the heat of the season in your retreat at Careggi, you will perhaps think the shelter of Fiesole not undeserving of your notice. Seated between the sloping sides of the mount, here we have water in abundance and, being constantly refreshed with moderate winds, find little inconvenience from the glare of the sun. As you approach the house it seems surrounded by trees, but when you reach it, you find it commands a full prospect of the city. Populous as the vicinity is, I can enjoy here that solitude so gratifying to my disposition.

ANGELO POLIZIANO TO MARSILIO FICINO

The most attractive spot to enjoy the incomparable view over Florence is the village of Fiesole, just beyond the northern limit of the city. Lorenzo's uncle Giovanni spotted the area's potential and asked Michelozzo to build him a delightful villa where he could escape the sounds and smells of the city. Lorenzo's friends love Fiesole and two of them, Pico della Mirandola and Angelo Poliziano, live here.

Fiesole is quite a cultural centre. Together with the neighbouring villages of Settignano and Maiano it has produced many of the best sculptors to work in Florence during the past century (Mino da Fiesole, Desiderio da Settignano, and the brothers Benedetto and Giuliano da Maiano). There are numerous churches, notably San Domenico, where the great Archbishop Antonino and the painter Fra Angelico served as novices. Strange to think that these truly holy men were living in close proximity to a nest of unbelievers who were practising the dark arts – at least if gossip about the village being a centre of sorcery is true (see p. 100).

MEDICI VILLAS

Yesterday after leaving Florence we came as far as San Miniato, singing all the way, and occasionally talking of holy things so as not to forget Lent. At Lastra we drank zappolino, which tasted much better than I had been told. Lorenzo is brilliant and makes the whole company gay.

ANGELO POLIZIANO

Lorenzo is a great lover of the countryside and is never happier than when escaping from the city to ride into more remote villages, dining with the locals on pickled meats, boiled fowl and other delicacies, washed down with quantities of Trebbiano wine. Lorenzo is also an extremely talented poet, and glories in the beauties of the Tuscan countryside. He has written many delightful sonnets, filled with charming images:

A green meadow with
  beautiful flowers,
A flowing stream circling the
  growing grass,
A little bird, sadly singing of love,
Will far better appease every desire

LORENZO DE' MEDICI

The Villa Medici at Fiesole is just one of many owned by the family. The original power base of the Medici was in the Mugello, a couple of hours' ride north of Florence and the family owns a number of fine houses among the hills including the fortified villas of Trebbio and Careggi. Cosimo de' Medici used to come to Careggi 'to refresh his soul', as he put it, by pruning his vines. His grandson Lorenzo has installed the Platonic Academy here, and encourages leading humanists to come to gain intellectual refreshment and enrichment. On the anniversary of Plato's birthday, 7 November, nine select members gather here to honour the great man's memory. This often takes place in the villa of Marsilio Ficino. Frequent attendees are the poets Angelo Poliziano and Luigi Pulci, Pico della Mirandola, and the mathematician and cartographer Paolo Toscanelli. Parts of Plato's *Symposium* are read, and songs sung, accompanied by the musician Antonio Squarcialupi

The Neo-Platonism that Lorenzo and his friends espouse is a combination of Greek philosophy and Christianity. They believe that it is the power of love that lifts the soul towards heaven. This may sound a bit esoteric but a number of artists, notably Botticelli, have been inspired by these ideas to produce some masterpieces. At Spedalotto, another Medici villa, for instance, you can admire magnificent frescoes Lorenzo has recently commissioned from Botticelli, his star pupil Filippino Lippi, Ghirlandaio and Pietro Perugino, fresh from their triumph in painting the walls of the Sistine Chapel in the Vatican.

Lorenzo's favourite project at the moment is the villa he is constructing at Poggio a Caiano, just south of Prato. He is never happier than when discussing plans with his architect Giuliano da Sangallo, although Lorenzo's recent illness means that he visits the villa much less often than he would wish. The building has certainly impressed contemporaries. Sangallo has come up with the highly original design that looks like an antique villa with a classical temple front, something that has not been seen since the time of the ancient Romans.

As well as being a place of pleasure, Poggio a Caiano is also the centre of a large agricultural enterprise, a working farm where Lorenzo is always trying to make improvements. He knows the value of the silk industry and has just planted a number of mulberry trees to produce silk for the looms of Florence. When he comes here, Lorenzo loves to talk to the local peasants and learns from them the practicalities of farming. In the evening, if he is alone, Lorenzo will write poetry, inspired by his love of the countryside, or improvise on the lyre. He sheds his *lucco* in favour of cheaper and more comfortable woollen clothes from the Casentino valley.

Lorenzo now rarely rides out hawking. He likes to wander round his garden, planted with box and myrtle hedges, and to show his friends the exotic additions to his menagerie: golden pheasants from Sicily, gazelles from Tunis, apes, parrots and a giraffe given to him by the Sultan of Babylon.

Botticelli's beautiful painting of Flora presiding over the Garden of Love.

Lorenzo is very proud of the horses bred here, some intended for racing, others to be presented as diplomatic gifts. Rulers all over Italy and beyond value horses very highly, and they assume great importance in the diplomatic manoeuvring of which Lorenzo is such a master.

Other members of the Medici family have properties out here. Lorenzo's cousins, Lorenzo di Pierfrancesco and Giovanni di Pierfrancesco are now installed at Castello, after winning a bitter court case against Lorenzo in which they successfully accused him of denying them their inheritance. (Lorenzo was forced to sell his beloved Caffagiolo, where he had spent many

of his happiest hours in childhood.) If you would like to visit Castello, speak to Amerigo Vespucci, a close friend of Lorenzo di Pierfrancesco. Although Amerigo has acquired a reputation as a wheeler-dealer, he is a brilliant and cultured man, and more importantly, his family owns a marvellous painting by Botticelli of Mars and Venus. As a result, he may well be receptive if you ask to see the two Botticellis owned by Lorenzo di Pierfrancesco. Those who have seen them say that they are two of the most beautiful paintings in Italy. One depicts the naked figure of Venus standing on a shell, being blown to the shore; the other is an allegorical scene featuring three dancing woman and beside them a beautiful woman strewing flowers.

TOWN VERSUS COUNTRY

*t is quite incredible how much malice
here is in these ploughboys who have
grown up among the clods. All their
efforts are directed towards fooling you;
ut they never let themselves be fooled
y anything.... If the harvest is good,
ie will keep the best share to himself.
f, because of bad weather or some other
eason, the fields are barren this year,
he peasant will not let you have any-
hing but damage and losses.*

ALBERTI, *TREATISE ON THE FAMILY*

The government acknowledges the
close relationship Florentines have
with the countryside and suspends its
activities during August and September so that citizens can leave town to
visit their properties in the country.
Many Florentines own land within
easy distance of the city and take a
keen interest in their farms. These are
usually leased to peasant farmers on
a crop-sharing basis, known as the
mezzadria. This is intended to give the
farmer the incentive to maximize his
profit, and, when you go out into the
countryside, you will see how inten-
sively much of the land is cultivated.
Olives and vines are staple crops, the
rows between planted with corn and
vegetables, and there are numerous
sheep and pigs roaming in the less
productive woods and uplands. Being
a frugal race, Florentines make sure
that all the produce from their farms
is used. Not only do they eat it themselves but they are also happy to make
payments in kind. Take the example
of the smith Masi who pays a rent of 15
florins per year for his house and shop,
plus a goose on All Saints Day and a
brace of capons at Carnival.

Nevertheless, despite the admirable
way that the Medici and the Rucellai
treat their tenants, there is an under-

*Ambrogio Lorenzetti depicts the benefits
of peace in the city and the surrounding
countryside.*

lying suspicion between town and country. It is hard work being a farmer, especially if you are dependent on the city for your livelihood. The peasant farmer does not own the land he farms and is therefore in the hands of the owner, who may well be unsympathetic to his predicament. The prices for his crops are set in the markets of Florence and are beyond his control. He does not even benefit personally from this, as the most nutritious crops, wheat, rye and millet, go to the city, and he and his family have to eat barley, vetch and inferior grains.

If you have the opportunity to talk to peasants on your travels, you will find that they grumble that they have no say over taxation, which is set by a government that panders to urban interests. The countryside is a dangerous place, with bands of mercenaries terrorizing farmers and robbing travellers. If there is a war, it is they who suffer most, their crops destroyed by invading armies, their goods seized their houses looted and their wive raped. No wonder so many peasant leave the countryside for the safet of the city, where they can dream o making their fortune.

If peasants are resentful of city folk the suspicion is entirely mutual. Man Florentines imagine that countrymen are a boorish lot, existing on a meagr diet consisting of soup, lots of garli and warmed-up cabbage. They regard them as a rough lot, prone to bloo feuds, livestock raids, boundary dis putes and vendettas. These illiterat peasants will take advantage of yo if you give them half a chance and must be kept in their place. Ales sandra Strozzi, usually a sympatheti character, writes dismissively: 'I hav flooded the field for next year, and as must have it put in order, these two ol people [Piero and Monna Cilia] mus go and beg, if they do not die. Heaven will provide.'

X · TOURING TUSCANY

Arezzo · Cortona · Prato · Lucca · Pisa
San Gimignano · Siena · Pienza

Now that you have sampled the delights of Florence, you will probably want to see what else Tuscany has to offer. This chapter offers three possible itineraries: east to the old Etruscan cities of Arezzo and Cortona; west down the Arno valley to prosperous Prato, Lucca and Pisa; and south along the via Cassia to sample the beauties of San Gimignano, Siena and Pienza. A word of advice whichever of these itineraries you follow: when you talk to the locals, avoid comparing their towns with Florence, they are universally touchy on the subject. And there is really no need, you will find the local festivals extremely exciting and the works of art of the highest quality. Every Tuscan is proud of the achievements of his fellow countrymen, and with complete justification.

AREZZO

Arezzo has a rather tricky relationship with Florence. The city has produced a remarkable number of famous men in recent times, but they always seem to go off to make their names in the larger city – much to the chagrin of the Aretines. Even in antiquity Maecenas, the great artistic patron in the time of Augustus, soon left Arezzo for the

bright lights of Rome. Petrarch, one of the great names in Italian literature, was born here, but his reputation rests on his inclusion in the Florentine literary pantheon alongside Dante and Boccaccio. Two of the leading statesmen and eminent humanists in Florence earlier this century, Leonardo Bruni and Carlo Marsuppini, were both from Arezzo but served as Chancellors to the Republic, and are buried in splendid tombs in Santa Croce. Indeed, Bruni wrote his celebrated *Lauditio* in praise not of his home town but of his adopted one.

In return, at least until Florence conquered Arezzo in 1384, the city played host to numerous exiles, including Dante, who took refuge here after he backed the wrong side in a civil war between two factions of the Guelph party. Today most Florentines who visit Arezzo cannot help but agree with Gentile Becchi (a recent Bishop of Arezzo and former tutor of Lorenzo) that the city is very provincial and a cultural backwater.

GIOSTRA DEL SARACINO

There are moments, however, when even the most jaded Florentine cannot help but enjoy life in Arezzo. Dante included a mention of the tournaments here in his *Inferno* and no wonder – the *Giostra del Saracino*, held on important feast days in the Piazza Grande, is one of the most exciting festivals in all Italy. It dates back to the time of the Crusades and takes its name from a wooden effigy, known as a *quintain*, in the form of a Saracen.

First of all, four groups, representing the four quarters of the city, process to the Cathedral, where they are blessed by the bishop; they then enter the steeply sloping Piazza Grande. Each group consists of a captain and four knights on horseback, armed with lanes and splendidly attired; they are accompanied by footmen, standard bearers, bowmen, halberdiers, drummers and trumpeters. Each quarte has its own colours: red and green fo Porta Crucifera, blue and yellow fo Porta Santo Spirito, green and whit for Porta Sant'Andrea, crimson an yellow for Porta del Foro.

At a sign from the Master of th Field, who holds a golden lance, th knights level their lances and charge i turn at the effigy. The effigy (which i also known as the King of the Indies o *Buratto*) holds a target in the shape o a shield in one hand, and in the othe three cords with leather balls fille with lead. Points are awarded if th contestant strikes the shield, particu larly if he breaks his lance, but deducte if he is struck by the leather balls The crowd is very partisan, cheerin, wildly when their champion is success ful and laughing uproariously if on of the rival knights is unseated by th Saracen. When the jousting is over, th winner is awarded the golden lance.

THREAT FROM THE EAST

The Tuscans still remember the Crusades, and the threat posed by the Saracen armies who recaptured the Holy Land remains very real. Just ten years ago, when the Republic of Florence was fighting the kingdom of Naples, and Lorenzo de' Medici had bravely gone to plead his case with King Ferrante, his life may well have been saved by the sudden appearance of a Turkish fleet off Otranto, in the heel of Italy. The Turks captured the port, massacring the Christians and forcing Ferrante to make a hasty peace with Lorenzo so that he could deal with the Muslim forces that had appeared so unexpectedly.

PIERO DELLA FRANCESCA

You will hardly have come acros the name of Piero della Francesca i Florence, but he is far and away th greatest painter from this area (ignor Florentines who maintain that Pier only came to work here because h could not obtain any decent commis sions in Florence). In fact Piero is stil living nearby in Borgo Sansepolcro although he is very infirm, and gav up painting many years ago when hi eyesight began to fail.

The grace of the Queen of Sheba shows why Piero della Francesca rivals the best Florentine painters.

The Franciscans are custodians of the holy sites in Jerusalem, and they like to emphasize this fact – hence the name of their main church in Florence, Santa Croce (Holy Cross). So it was only natural that Francesco Bacci and his son Giovanni, whose family used the chancel of San Francesco as a funerary chapel, would commission Piero to paint the *Legend of the True Cross* there, enabling viewers to make a vicarious trip to Jerusalem.

Locals regard the austere, monumental figures in these frescoes as superior to anything executed by Piero's contemporaries in Florence, though he was clearly inspired by Masaccio's frescoes in the Brancacci Chapel. They will draw your attention to the beautiful group of the Queen of Sheba and her maidens and a wonderful nocturnal scene of the Emperor Constantine lying asleep with his attendant keeping watch. They will

point out that the best way to appreciate the frescoes is to look at them in pairs: two battle scenes at the bottom, then above them two scenes of the discovery of the Cross (by the Queen of Sheba and St Helena), and, at the top, the death of Adam and the exaltation of the Cross.

Piero was born not far away, in Borgo Sansepolcro, whose name derives from two relics of the Holy Sepulchre carried back by pilgrims from the Holy Land six centuries ago. The civic symbol of the town is the Risen Christ and in the town hall Piero has painted a marvellous fresco of the *Resurrection*, with Christ stepping out of the tomb in the dawn light while four soldiers lie sleeping at his feet (one of these guards bears Piero's self-portrait). As a tribute to his mother, Piero painted the *Madonna del Parto* in a little chapel in the village of Monterchi where she is buried. It is one of his most beautiful paintings, with two angels drawing aside a curtain to reveal the pregnant Madonna, who has tears on her cheeks in the knowledge of the tragedy that will befall her son.

CORTONA

Half a day's ride south of Arezzo lies the hilltop eyrie of Cortona. Like Arezzo, Cortona was one of the twelve cities of the Etruscan confederation, a power in central Italy long before Florence even existed. The town certainly occupies a wonderful site, with panoramic views over Lake Trasimene. It was here that Hannibal achieved one of his most spectacular victories, completely annihilating a Roman army beside the lake. So bloody was the battle that a couple of villages below Cortona are named Ossaia (bones) and Sanguineta (blood) in memory of the event; even today peasant farmers ploughing their fields occasionally uncover the remains of an unfortunate legionary.

There is plenty to see in Cortona. Locals are very proud of the painter Luca Signorelli, whose works, with their muscular figures, can be seen in many of the town's churches. They make quite a contrast with a beautiful and graceful *Annunciation* Fra Angelico painted for the church of San Domenico. But the main reason to visit Cortona is to join the throng of pilgrims who flock to the site of a miraculous appearance of an image of the Virgin in a tannery just outside the walls. Francesco di Giorgio, the greatest Sienese architect, has been awarded the commission to build a church on the site to accommodate the faithful. The miraculous appearance has sparked large pilgrimages, and the Cortonesi are anxious to cater to the pilgrims' needs by giving them accommodation and sustenance after their long journey – making a decent profit in the process.

PRATO

The town of Prato lies a couple of hours' ride west of Florence. You can either visit the town on a day trip from Florence, or spend the night in an inn such as the Albergo della Stella. Prato's proximity to its powerful neighbour and its dependence on the cloth trade has meant that the town has rarely escaped Florence's influence. Once when news of a riot in Prato reached Lorenzo, Florentine troops arrived in the main square to quell the disturbance within hours.

Prato is home to a unique and particularly sacred relic, the Virgin's girdle. If you visit Prato on 8 September, the feast of the Virgin, you will struggle to enter the Piazza del Duomo so great are the crowds that come to see this relic displayed from the pulpit outside the Cathedral. Come back another day to admire the pulpit, which was specially built for the purpose by Michelozzo and decorated with a frieze of angels by Donatello. Inside the Cathedral you can visit the chapel where the girdle is normally housed. If you want to see something less celestial, have a look at the frescoes in the choir by Filippo Lippi. An appreciative audience, led by King Herod and including Carlo de' Medici, illegitimate son of Cosimo and provost of the Cathedral, are transfixed by the dancing figure of Salomé, who has long since cast aside her girdle. Filippo should know about such things, since the model for Salomé was his wife Lucrezia (the same who had previously appeared as the Virgin – see p. 67).

Because of their precious relic, the Pratesi are especially devoted to the Virgin. Following her miraculous appearance in a prison six years ago, the locals have commissioned the church of Santa Maria dei Carceri to house the throngs of pilgrims who have flocked to the site. Anxious to please Lorenzo de' Medici, they have asked the great man's advice; he has recommended Giuliano da Sangallo, who is currently working at Poggio a Caiano.

HOLY GIRDLE

You may be wondering how Prato came to possess the Virgin's girdle. On her Assumption, the Virgin bequeathed the item to St Thomas; he in turn left it in the Holy Land. Centuries later, when a certain Michele from Prato became engaged to a girl called Maria in Jerusalem, he was most surprised when she gave it to him as her dowry. Much gratified, on returning to Prato, Michele took to hiding the girdle under his mattress, much to the annoyance of watching angels who threw him out of his bed whenever he did so. Suitably chastened, Michele presented the girdle to the Cathedral on his death in 1174. A special chapel was built to house it, guarded by both the church and the commune, each of whom was given a key. If you go to see it, you will join an illustrious list of visitors including St Francis of Assisi, St Bernardino of Siena, Pope Alexander V and the Byzantine Emperor John Paleologus.

Two prosperous-looking bankers from Prato are seated at a table, ready to commence the day's business.

A view of Prato with a group of horsemen approaching the city walls.

Pistoia, the next major town to the west, is of considerably less interest. It is famous for the production of small daggers known as *pistole*, a suitable industry considering the town's reputation for violence.

LUCCA

As at Prato the most remarkable object in Lucca is a religious relic, the Volto Santo (Holy Face). This wooden crucifix, which shows the image of the Saviour, was supposedly carved by Nicodemus, who had helped lift Christ's body down from the Cross. The fame of this relic and the miracles it works are so great that in faraway England the Norman king William Rufus used to swear oaths *per sanctum*

Vultum de Luca (by the holy face of Lucca). The locals, anxious to promote their town as a place of pilgrimage (and in the process benefit the local economy), have placed the image on Lucca's coins.

The Volto Santo is housed in Lucca Cathedral in a special *tempietto* recently completed by the highly talented local sculptor and architect Matteo Civitali. When you visit, you will be sure to find a number of devout believers praying in front of it. While you are in the Cathedral have a look at Jacopo della Quercia's beautiful tomb of Ilaria da Caretto, wife of Paolo Guinigi, ruler of Lucca back in 1400, just round the corner. The most important day in the Lucchese calen-

The precious Volto Santo in Lucca Cathedral, widely believed to have been carved by Nicodemus himself.

dar is 13 September, when the Volto Santo is lifted with great care onto a cart and paraded in triumph round the city. The procession winds its way through the streets, passing by the church of San Michele in Foro, with the commanding figure of St Michael slaying the dragon standing on top of its richly decorated façade. This was once the Roman Forum, the site of a famous meeting between Caesar, Pompey and Crassus, the three greatest Romans of the day.

You may well be wondering how such a small town has maintained its independence – particularly when you hear how dearly Florentines would like to take revenge for the humiliation they suffered early last century when the Lucchese general Castruccio Castracani almost captured their city. The answer is that Lucca is very rich: its citizens have made a great deal of money from pilgrims passing down the via Francigena, and its merchants, with all the profits they have gained from the silk trade, have paid for the impressive set of fortifications that today encircles the town. So strong are these walls that not even the Florentines have dared to assault them.

PISA

There is nothing new here, except that in the neighbourhood of Pisa, where the illustrious Lorenzo is hawking with King Ferrante's men, two of the falcons sent by His Majesty, and those the best, are lost.

A REPORT BY AN AMBASSADOR TO
THE DUKE OF FERRARA

LOCAL RIVALRIES

After Nicodemus carved the Volto Santo he cast it into the sea. Much later, in the 8th century, it landed on the coast of Tuscany. The inhabitants of Lucca and Luni in Liguria both immediately claimed possession of the holy image. The Bishop of Lucca was invited to settle the dispute, and to show his impartiality, he ordered the sculpture to be loaded onto an ox cart – the oxen would decide where to take the piece, and they headed straight for Lucca. It was then housed in the church of San Frediano but was moved to the Cathedral on its consecration in 1070.

Pisans dream of the past. They are immensely proud of their city and its history, and still look back to the days when the Pisan Maritime Republic owned the islands of Sardinia and Corsica, and was one of the leading powers in the Mediterranean, with extensive trading outposts stretching from the Balearic Islands in the west to Syria in the east. Her navies vied with the Genoese, the Venetians and the Saracens, while her armies defied Florence and Lucca with impunity. This is but a distant memory: Pisa has been under Florentine control for the past eighty years. Lorenzo de' Medici realizes that many Pisans still feel bitter about their loss of independence and has done his best to promote Pisa. He has worked hard to construct a canal to prevent the Arno silting up, which would be a disaster for the port at Pisa as well as for Florentine trade.

PIAZZA DEI MIRACOLI

Locals will be swift to tell you that they possess a collection of buildings that are a miracle in themselves, far superior to anything down the road in Lucca. They are so impressive that they have named the surrounding area the Piazza dei Miracoli. Four gleaming white marble structures stand in this piazza: the Cathedral, Baptistery, campanile and Camposanto, all dating from the 11th to 13th centuries, the greatest era in the city's history. The fortunes made by Pisan merchants paid for these wonderful buildings though nobody can agree whether this style of building with striped marble, blind arcading and a mass of sculptural decoration originated with the architecture of Pisa's Saracen enemies, or in Lombardy, or even in Constantinople.

No sooner had the Cathedral been completed in the 12th century than it was decided to build the Baptistery in the same style. The style proved so popular that it has since been imitated all over Tuscany, especially in the churches of Lucca, Pistoia, Prato and Arezzo, and even in the Cathedral in Siena and the Baptistery in Florence. Typical, Pisans scoff, that their neighbours are unable to create a decent architecture of their own. The craze for striped marble has also spread to Puglia and to the islands of Elba, Corsica and Sardinia. The campanile is an even bigger attraction. Pisans take a perverse pride in the fact that it looks as though it is about to topple over, and enjoy the story of the hunchback Giovanni from Innsbruck, one of the original masons back in the late 13th century, who designed it to lean in revenge for his deformity.

The fourth building on the Piazza dei Miracoli is the Camposanto, a cemetery filled with earth brought back from the Holy Land in 1200 by Archbishop Lanfranchi. This holy earth has special powers and, like some form of celestial compost, turns a corpse into a skeleton within a matter of days. The walls are decorated with frescoes, including some by Benozzo Gozzoli. Other, earlier, frescoes show vivid representations of the *Triumph of Death,* the *Crucifixion,* the *Last Judgment* and *Hell* – these were painted immediately after the Black Death when the full horror of the event was still fresh in the memory. Whatever you do, don't ask to see the chains that once closed the Pisa harbour. They used to hang here but were carried off by the Genoese back in 1362, a terrible humiliation.

PISAN SCULPTORS

Pisans are justifiably proud of their two greatest sculptors, both of whom have taken their names from their adopted city. Nicola Pisano, originally from Puglia in the heel of Italy, came to work in Pisa back in the 13th century. His finest work is the pulpit in the Baptistery where the figures are strongly influenced by the art of antiquity.

Nicola's chief assistant was his son Giovanni, who carved an equally beautiful pulpit for the Cathedral at the beginning of the 14th century. Giovanni's figures, with their complex poses and expressive gestures, are more realistic than those of his father. The Pisani are a talented bunch, and

Nicola Pisano's splendid carving on the pulpit of the Baptistery in Pisa has inspired generations of Tuscan sculptors.

Andrea Pisano, another sculptor of the first rank, carved a fine set of doors for the Baptistery in Florence (the first set, not the ones that led to the row between Ghiberti and Brunelleschi). And the famous leaning tower was begun by someone called Bonnano Pisano back in 1173.

The Florentines, of course, refuse to concede any measure of cultural superiority to the Pisans. They regard Donatello's pulpits in San Lorenzo as superior to those of Nicola or Giovanni Pisano, and Ghiberti's doors for the Baptistery as much finer than those by Andrea Pisano. Moreover, the domes in the Piazza dei Miracoli bear no comparison with the one by Brunelleschi. As for painting in Pisa, just go to the church of Santa Maria del Carmine, south of the Arno, and admire Masaccio's altarpiece; no Pisan painter could even begin to compare with the achievement of this Florentine. (Clearly the order had a penchant for the artist, since the Brancacci Chapel in the order's church in Florence contains his greatest painting.)

FESTIVALS

The most exciting of all Pisan festivals is the Gioco del Ponte and if possible you should time your visit to coincide with it. There is a dress rehearsal known as the Battagliaccia on 17 January (the feast of St Anthony Abbot) but the main event, the Battaglia Generale, tends to take place whenever an important Florentine pays a visit (which is very galling for the Pisans). The whole city turns out to watch two teams fight for possession of one of the city's bridges, the Ponte di Mezzo. This is not for the faint-hearted, and if you feel squeamish you may want to concentrate on the spectacle of the costumed participants parading along the banks of the Arno. They carry banners representing the four quarters of the city: Santa Maria and San Francesco on the north bank of the Arno (known as the Tramontana), and San Martin and Sant' Antonino on the south bank (the Mezzogiorno).

The game is nicknamed *mazzascudo* (literally kill-shield) after a type of shield with a broad and a narrow end that can be used for both defence and attack. The winner is the first to gain full control of the bridge and no quarter is given. As well as the *targone* (as the shields are more commonly known), the two teams, in full armour, wield maces and cudgels. Many players are wounded, sometimes fatally. The winners are presented with the *palio* (pennant) which is handed over in the Palazzo Communale. It is said to date back to a famous incident in 1005, when Pisa was saved by the quick thinking of young Kinzica de' Sigismondi, who spotted the invading Saracens as they crept up to the walls by night and rang the church bells, thus giving the defenders time to man the battlements and repel them.

If you prefer something less violent, there is sometimes a regatta on the Arno. This used to be an annual event, a celebration of the city's great maritime history, held on 15 August (the feast of the Assumption). Now that Florence controls the city, however, there is little for the Pisans to celebrate. The race itself is very exciting, as the rowers demonstrate their strength and skill. Traditionally, the winner is awarded a banner while the loser is given a gosling.

THE UNIVERSITY OF PISA AND THE MEDICI

On my return from the country, I heard that you had gone to Pisa and that, on your instruction, I had been appointed one of the new governors of the University. I thank you for the post, for I am delighted to have it, particularly as I shall be serving in your company.

DONATO ACCAIUOLI TO LORENZO DE' MEDICI,
SEPTEMBER 1473

If you want to study law, medicine and theology, the University of Pisa has replaced that of Florence as the place to go (its university dates back to the last century). In large part this is due to the patronage of Lorenzo de' Medici, who wants to raise the profile of the university and has encouraged notable academics (including Bartolomeo Sozzini, an eminent lawyer from the University in Bologna) to come to teach here.

You can tell how seriously Lorenzo takes this from the amount of time he has spent in Pisa. On one occasion he even missed an important family gathering on All Saints Day. Lorenzo's mother wrote sadly to him: 'We are sending, by Maso de Ciave, your share of the feast so that you can enjoy it with your friends. We send geese, chestnuts and ravioli...we wish you would come home.' Lorenzo's brother Giuliano studied here, although he preferred to enjoy the good things in life, writing to his mother in May 1474: 'We have arrived safely and are well, today we dance, and tomorrow we joust, which, as is the custom of this country, should be fine.' Hearing how enjoyable it is, many Florentines have followed Giuliano's example and come to study at the university.

SAN GIMIGNANO

San Gimignano seems terribly old-fashioned. All those towers that dominate the skyline hark back to an earlier era when every town in Tuscany resembled a petrified forest. Local ladies can see no point in them: they are hopelessly impractical, their slaves can't climb up all those stairs with the shopping, and in any case the days when the owners climbed to the top and hurled stones down onto neighbours are well and truly over. Why can't they live in civilized houses like they do in Florence? If you talk to one of the husbands, however – especially if he owns one of

the highest towers – he may have a different view. His house is visible to all, and clients and friends alike can see that he is an important member of the community.

Status is important in San Gimignano. The town stands on the via Francigena, the important pilgrimage road connecting France and Rome. The pilgrims are a varied lot, ranging from rich merchants with caravans in tow to poor, ragged figures, armed only with a walking stick, looking for the cheapest hostel in town. The locals have made a lot of money from this passing trade and you can still see the symbols of the Templar and Hospitaller orders on houses where they put up pilgrims during the era of the Crusades.

San Gimignano is also a centre of the textile trade. If you visit in springtime, you will see the fields surrounding the town filled with yellow crocuses that produce a saffron dye, crucial to the cloth trade in Florence. The actual method of producing this dye is a closely guarded secret. Alternatively, visit during the wine harvest in the autumn, when you can taste the excellent Vernaccia wine, a great favourite of Lorenzo de' Medici and of Pope Martin IV, who loved to eat eels that had been soaked in the wine before roasting them over a charcoal fire.

San Gimignano stands very near the southern frontier of the Florentine Republic, and has every need of its impressive walls. To show their loyalty, the citizens have commissioned some major works of art recently by Florentine artists (earlier works were commissioned from Sienese painters, when Siena held the town). The finest frescoes in the Cathedral, known as the Collegiata, are by Domenico Ghirlandaio, in a beautiful chapel designed by Giuliano da Maiano. They tell the story of the life of St Fina, a famously virtuous and ascetic girl who, to her parents' bafflement, insisted on sleeping on a wooden board.

At her death her wooden board suddenly sprouted violets. There were more excitements at the saint's funeral, when a nurse miraculously

The forest of towers has made the skyline of San Gimignano one of the most famous in all Tuscany.

regained the use of her paralysed hand and a clerk regained his sight. If you look closely at the funeral scene Ghirlandaio chose to depict himself his brother David and his brother-in-law Sebastiano Mainardi in attendance – though of course the actual events took place two hundred years before Ghirlandaio.

Ghirlandaio was following in the footsteps of Benozzo Gozzoli who also worked extensively in San Gimignano. Gozzoli's figures are eternal optimists. Take his St Sebastian, in the Collegiata. Blissfully unaware of his impending martyrdom, the saint stares fixedly out of the painting while archers fire arrows at such a rate that his unprotected body resembles a pincushion. At the other end of town Gozzoli painted scenes from the life

Benozzo Gozzoli's scenes from the life of St Augustine are full of humorous details; here, while Augustine sets off for school, our eye is diverted by a squealing, bare-bottomed baby.

You have great abundance in grain and wine,
Nor do you lack splendour and a pleni-tude of riches.
How shall I be silent about your beauti-ful women, famous throughout the world?
Who can count the number of your airy towers?
Live a long, happy life, and may all things be favourable for you!
I pray that you be happy, venerable city of the life-giving Virgin.

PAEAN ON THE FEAST OF THE ASSUMPTION, 1484

of St Augustine in the chancel of the church of Sant' Agostino. In these the saint shows no concern that he will soon bear the weight of the early Church on his shoulders as he sets off to school, stands nonchalantly while a retainer divests him of his spurs, and rides through a Tuscan landscape accompanied by his friends.

SIENA

Ancient Siena, called city of the life-giving Virgin,
Light, honour and lustre of all Italy:
Yours is the precious gift of innate liberty,
And yours is continuing and unceasing peace.
You excel by your zeal for virtue; glory and renown
Make you illustrious; you are above all others in talent.

It is impossible not to be seduced by Siena. The beauty of the city, particularly the Campo, with the battlements of the Palazzo Pubblico (the town hall and seat of government) rising up like a castle in a fairytale, and the lyricism and elegance of the paintings of Duccio and Simone Martini, are irresistible. If you hire a guide to take you round the city, you will find that he reinforces this view by dwelling on a golden age in the early 14th century, when the government of the Council of Nine (the *Noveschi*) encouraged trade and instigated a programme of good works, making sure the streets were clean and the water supply plentiful. Siena was then one of the greatest cities in Europe, with famous artists and superb buildings, notably the Cathedral and Palazzo Pubblico. Her merchant-bankers brought prosperity to the city, and for a time it really seemed true that Siena was the heir to

Rome. In fact, the city's emblem is the she-wolf, since the Sienese claim that the city was founded by the twin sons of Remus – which means, of course, that it is much older than Florence.

Your guide will also stress that the Sienese are an intensely religious people. They take great pride in their compatriots St Catherine and St Bernardino, two of the most important saints in all Italy, far more important than any to have come from Florence. St Catherine played a vital role in the late 14th century in persuading the pope of the day to return to Rome from exile in Avignon. She was a figure of such holiness that she imagined that she had entered a mystical marriage with Christ (this has since become a favourite subject of painters). Earlier this century, St Bernardino, despite his unprepossessing appearance, with his hollow cheeks, down-turned mouth and pointed chin, became the greatest preacher in Tuscany.

The noted Sienese humanist Aeneas Silvius Piccolomini was elected Pope Pius II in 1458 and erected some fine buildings in his home town, easily recognized by the family's emblem of the crescent moon. In contrast there has never been a Florentine pope, though they treated the self-styled John XXIII back in the 1420s as one of their own (even though there was a canonically elected pope sitting in Rome), burying him in their Baptistery in an ostentatious monument designed by Donatello.

What your guide will be less keen to discuss is current affairs and you may have to treat him first to a glass of wine and a *panpepato* (a delicious Sienese speciality). There are good contemporary things to talk about first: a number of fine new palaces have been built, the Monte dei Paschi bank (founded in 1472) is thriving, Siena's university continues to flourish, the study of humanism (which has been so stimulating in Florentine life) thrives, and a printing press has recently opened in the city. But there are also major causes for concern. The wool and banking trades are in severe decline, and a new regime led by Pandolfo Pandolfini has just seized power. The government he ousted had been in alliance with Florence and the Sienese are fearful that Lorenzo de' Medici will intervene – he likes nothing better than to encourage fighting between factions to keep Siena disunited, ensuring that it poses no threat to Florence. The Sienese are determined to maintain their independence and are perennially afraid (not without justification) that their northern neighbour has designs on the city. If your guide hears that you have just visited Florence, he will be reluctant to talk about current affairs. He will undoubtedly prefer to talk about the Palio about which every Sienese is passionate (see below).

THE CULT OF THE VIRGIN

, most miserable and unfaithful of sin-
-ers give, donate and concede to you
his city of Siena and all its contado, *its*
military] force and its district, and as a
ign of this I place the keys of the city of
iena on this altar.

PAOLO DI TOMMASO MONTAURI RECORDS THE
WORDS OF BUONAGUIDA LUCARI, HEAD OF
THE SIENESE GOVERNMENT, WHO PROCESSED
TO THE CATHEDRAL, BAREFOOT AND WITH
A HALTER ROUND HIS NECK, BEFORE
THE BATTLE OF MONTAPERTI

THE BATTLE OF MONTAPERTI

The most important date in Sienese
history is 4 September 1260, when
the outnumbered Sienese army won
a famous victory over the hated
Florentines at the Battle of Montaperti.
The night before the battle, a great light
illuminated the Sienese camp and the
devout soldiers fervently believed that it
was the Virgin who was covering them
with her mantle and taking them under
her protection. At dawn the Sienese
attacked with such ferocity that the
Florentine army was utterly destroyed.
The Sienese captured a cart filled
with gold coins (money used by
the Florentines to pay mercenaries),
and the arrogant Florentine
ambassador (who just a few days
before had demanded Siena's
surrender) was led back into the
city at the head of a triumphant
procession, mounted backwards
on an ass.

The momentous victory at the Battle
of Montaperti greatly increased the
Sienese devotion to the Virgin. There
are numerous images of her in the city,
including two over the gates of Porta
Camollia and Porta Romana, placed
specifically at the points of maximum
danger to help to repel attackers.

The Cathedral is dedicated to the
Virgin, and the principal public ceremony is the feast of the Assumption
(16 August). On the preceding evening,
the chief magistrates hold a banquet at
the Palazzo Pubblico for representatives of subject territories. The next
morning they all process to the Cathedral in their most splendid robes, followed by lords of the castles conquered
by the Sienese, bearing wax candles,
which are offered to the Queen of
Heaven (the largest candle weighs
a hefty 100 pounds). The shops are
closed and the day is given up to feast-
ing and enjoyment, with jousting and
the Palio (see p. 135) run through the
streets. During the three-day festival
everyone looks their smartest, servants are given new livery and women
are permitted to wear their finest silk
and velvet dresses in public.

As in Florence the government has
done its best to prevent the Sienese
from spending too much on clothes
and jewelry. Locals remember what
consternation Battista Petrucci caused
when the Emperor Federick III and
his bride-to-be Leonora of Portugal
visited in 1452. The emperor was so
impressed with Battista's recitation in

Latin that he offered her any reward she cared to name – to which she begged to be allowed to ignore all regulations on dress. It required all the emperor's efforts to persuade the government to give way on this.

THE CAMPO

[The Campo] is held to be one of the most beautiful squares which can be seen not only in Italy but in the whole of Christendom, both for the loveliness of the fountain and for the beauty of the buildings which surround it.

A CHRONICLER IN 1347

The first place to visit, and undoubt edly the most beautiful spot in Siena is the Campo. This main square stand at the junction of Siena's three hills with the Palazzo Pubblico as its foca point. Locals wax lyrical, with com plete justification, over the shape o the Campo, likening it to a shell or fan. It slopes down to the Fonte Gaia a much-admired fountain carved b Jacopo della Quercia at the begin ning of the century. Every mornin a market is held in the Campo – her you will find the Sienese buying thei fruit and vegetables (if you want t buy some livestock, you must go dow to the Fontebranda). On importar

The Campo in Siena with the slender tower of the Mangia rising high above the Palazzo Pubblico.

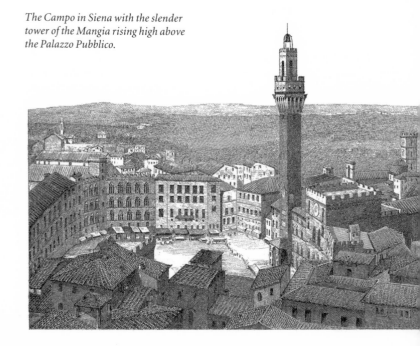

religious occasions you may see a famous preacher delivering a sermon on a platform outside the Palazzo Pubblico, following a tradition started by St Bernardino, who used to attract vast crowds when he preached here; his monogram IHS in honour of Christ adorns the Palazzo Pubblico.

The Campo is the scene of public festivals, where foreign dignitaries are welcomed in great style. In 1467, Ippolita Maria Sforza, the Duke of Milan's daughter, arrived with a cavalcade of one thousand people en route to her marriage with the Duke of Calabria. At a ball in front of the Palazzo Pubblico a troop of dancing girls emerged from a golden she-wolf and sang a song of how they did not want to be nuns which brought a big cheer from the crowd. Recently the feast of St Mary Magdalene has been celebrated here since the Council of Nine returned to power on that day. Government ordinances are proclaimed and public executions carried out in the Campo – and if the citizens are discontented, this is the natural setting for a riot or protest against the government.

PALAZZO PUBBLICO

I see merchants buying and selling, I see dancing, the houses being repaired, the workers busy in the vineyards or sowing the fields, whilst on horseback others ride down to swim in the rivers; maidens I see going to a wedding, and great flocks of sheep and many another peaceful sight. Besides which I see a man hanging from the gallows, hung there in the cause of justice. And for the sake of these things men live in peace and harmony with one another.

ST BERNARDINO ON
AMBROGIO LORENZETTI'S *PEACE*

The exterior of the Palazzo Pubblico is an elegant concave façade with pointed arches and slender colonettes, built between the mid-13th and 14th centuries, when Siena was at the apogee of her power. It has served as a much-imitated prototype when the Sienese come to build their own palaces. Above it stands the Torre della Mangia, the home of the bell that regulates life in the city. It is rung four times a day, at dawn (when curfew ends and the city's gates are opened), at midday (a time for a meal and a break from work), at sunset, and once more three hours later (when curfew is reimposed). The Mangia bell is also rung in times of war or civic discord, and during festivals. The tower was only just completed when the Black Death struck Siena in 1348, wiping out over half of the population. Those with a clean bill of health can make the climb to the top, which offers a fantastic view over the Sienese countryside. The tower's name, by the way, comes from the nickname (*mangiaguadagni*, 'he who eats all he earns') given to the first bell-ringer, a well-known wastrel.

The interior of the Palazzo Pubblico is one of the wonders of Siena. Since

THE THREE HILLS

Siena's government is, to a large extent, determined by its geography. The city's three hills are known as the Terzo di Citta, the Terzo di Camollia and the Terzo di San Martino. So fundamental is this tripartite division that the government always consists of multiples of three – and when the Sienese go into battle their army is divided into three divisions, each wearing its own colours: green for Citta, black and white for Camollia, and red for San Martino.

its construction it has housed both the government and the treasury, known as the *Bicherna*. If you harbour any doubts about the merits of the great Sienese painters, this is where to put them to rest. There are two important rooms upstairs, the *Sala del Gran Consiglio* (Hall of the Great Council), and the *Sala delle Pace*, formerly the

Simone Martini's splendid painting of the Sienese general Guidoriccio da Foligno riding through the landscape.

armoury. They both have vast frescoes which make a fundamental point: if the government and the citizens play their part, all will be well, but if they do not, all will be chaos and the perpetrators will be punished. The frescoes were painted at the beginning of the last century, shortly after the palace was completed.

The Hall of the Great Council, also known as the *Sala del Mappamondo*, (after a rotating map of the world by Ambrogio Lorenzetti) has two vast frescoes by Simone Martini. On one wall, his *Maestà*, a depiction of the Virgin as Queen of Heaven, a favourite Sienese subject, depicts the graceful figure of the Madonna seated beneath a canopy borne by apostles and surrounded by angels. On the steps of her throne an inscription tells the rulers to govern wisely. On the opposite wall is an even more striking fresco, of Guidoriccio da Foligno, a noted *condottiere* and captain of the Sienese army, mounted on his splendidly attired horse, at the siege of Montemassi.

Next door, the *Sala della Pace* is where the government holds its meet-

ings. Enormous frescoes of *Peace and War* by Ambrogio Lorenzetti, commissioned by the Council of Nine, cover its entire walls. The contrast between the two opposing sides could not be starker: *Peace* shows a venerable old man, dressed in black and white (the colours of Siena), with the Virtues (notably Peace herself, dressed in white) and the more austere figure of Justice (seated on a throne and holding a pair of scales). The adjoining wall shows harmony within the city of Siena, while outside the city's walls peasants harvest the golden corn and the nobility set off to hunt wild boar. In *War*, however, figures of the Vices surround Lucifer, lord of the underworld, while anarchy prevails in the town: buildings collapse or are on fire, soldiers kill and maim at will and in the barren countryside villages are set ablaze.

THE CATHEDRAL AND BAPTISTERY

On the day when the new picture was brought to the Cathedral all the shops were locked up, the Bishop ordered a great and devoted company of priests and friars with a solemn procession, accompanied by the Signori of the Nine and all the officials of the Commune, and all the populace. All the most worthy were hand in hand next to the said panel with lights lit in their hands; and then behind were women and children with much devotion; and they accompanied it right to the Cathedral,

[processing] round the Campo, as was the custom, sounding all the bells in glory, out of devotion for such a noble panel as was this...

AN ANONYMOUS CHRONICLER ON THE
INSTALLATION OF DUCCIO'S *MAESTÀ*, 1311

The Sienese have devoted great love and care to their Cathedral. There is a hoard of relics, including the veil of the Virgin, a tooth of St Bernardino and – most precious of all – the arm of St John the Baptist. You can imagine how dearly the Florentines would love to possess the arm of their patron saint, which was given to Siena by Pope Pius II in 1464.

Over the high altar is installed Duccio's *Maestà*, a magnificent depiction of the Virgin as Queen of Heaven. It has two sides, one showing scenes from the life of Christ, the other (facing the congregation) showing scenes from the life of the Virgin. She is surrounded by the city's patron saints who are interceding on behalf of the Sienese.

Other works to admire are Nicola Pisano's pulpit, an exquisite piece of carving, executed just after the Battle of Montaperti, and the immensely complex and ornate façade by his son Giovanni. Few other artists from outside Siena have gained commissions in the building, though there are some fine works by Donatello, notably the relief he made for the font in the Baptistery (which is situated right beneath the east end of the Cathedral).

However, the Florentine failed to gain the commission for the door of the marble tabernacle of the font, which was instead awarded to a local goldsmith, Giovanni Turini.

The other marvel in the Cathedral is the extraordinary marble floor, which is still being constructed. This was the idea of Alberto Aringhieri, the Master of Works, and he has been busy commissioning all the best Sienese artists to make designs for sections of the pavement; their drawings are then carefully copied in marble by masons. The effect is very striking and, if you pay the sacristan a coin or two, you may even be allowed to see the masons at work. Every incentive is given to encourage the best workmen and artists. The Board of Works has even authorized for refreshment to be available because 'they cannot be expected to work all day without drinking', and one mason who had been banished from Siena for fornication has been allowed to return to work on the project.

The Sienese have, however, made one very costly mistake: early last century, desperate to surpass their Florentine rivals, they began a new and much larger Cathedral. Work had barely begun when there were major structural and financial problems, swiftly followed by the Black Death, putting an end to this hopelessly overambitious plan. You can still see the vast, unfinished arches extending out like a mutilated arm from the right transept.

THE HOSPITAL OF SANTA MARIA DELLA SCALA

Opposite the Cathedral stands the Hospital of Santa Maria della Scala, named after the flight of steps leading up to the façade. It is an ancient institution, at least 500 years old. It originally catered for the large number of pilgrims travelling along the via Francigena from France to Rome. There is an amusing fresco in the hospital depicting its legendary founder, the shoe-mender Sorore, whose mother had a dream of a ladder reaching up to heaven from this spot with little children ascending it into the arms of the Virgin. It is a fascinating place to visit, though ideally not as a patient.

Over the years the hospital has acquired numerous gifts from grateful patients, and it is now one of the richest institutions in the region, with property and branches throughout the Sienese Republic (and even one in Florence). The hospital has acquired relics from as far afield as Constantinople, including part of the Virgin's girdle and her veil, thus playing its part in promoting her cult. The Blessed Giovanni Colombini, originally a rich merchant and banker, was a major beneficiary. He gave most of his possessions to Santa Maria della Scala and became the founder of the Order of the Gesuati. When his wife, who was left with almost nothing, complained, Giovanni replied that she had always wanted him to be more charitable – to which she made the acid retort: 'I prayed for rain, not for the Flood.'

You may be fortunate enough to see the hospital's most precious relic, a nail from the cross on which Christ was crucified, which is housed in the Chapel of the Holy Nail. Even if this is off bounds, you can still visit the Room of the Pilgrims, which was frescoed fifty years ago by local artist Domenico di Bartolo with scenes of life in the hospital: feeding the poor, receiving orphans, caring for the sick and distributing alms.

THE PALIO AND OTHER FESTIVALS

He who has not seen the Palio does not know Siena.

SIENESE PROVERB

Orphans are well looked after in the Hospital of Santa Maria della Scala – this scene by Domenico di Bartolo depicts their reception, education and marriage.

Siena prides itself on its festivals which are very exciting, so be prepared. Most of them take place in the Campo. *Elmora*, an imitation battle, has now been replaced by *Pugna*, a legalized punch-up between two sides. Children indulge in a junior version with mock swords, known as *Giorgiani*, derived from the *giuochi giorgani* (an annual pageant on St George's Day celebrating the saint's assistance at the Battle of Montaperti). *Pallone* is a violent type of football that so excited the visiting Pope Gregory XII that he insisted – to the horror of his attendants – in joining in. A new excitement is bullfighting, which has brought in large crowds. Members of the districts of Siena, known as *contrade*, don elaborate costumes and create wooden structures in the shape of animals, which they shelter in while attempting to catch and kill the bulls.

Nothing, however, generates as much excitement as the Palio. This

CONTRADE

Originally there were 59 *contrade* (districts of the city). Each supplied troops for defence of the city, with the emblems of the *contrade* painted on the sides of the *caroccio* (war cart). Every Sienese soldier would rather die than see his *caroccio* fall into the hands of the enemy. In peacetime an eternal flame burns in front of it.

Today there are just seventeen main *contrade*, and members celebrate every major event – a baptism, a marriage, a death or a festival – in their own *contrada*. The greatest cause for celebration, however, is victory in the Palio, in which each *contrada* enters a horse.

The emblems of the modern *contrade* represent the seventeen Virtues of Siena: for example, the Panther symbolizes daring, the Giraffe elegance, the Snail prudence. The names of some of the *contrade* are quite comical: after all, it's difficult to imagine a race between a Caterpillar, a Snail and a Tortoise! Before you laugh too loudly, however, remember that the locals take the Palio very seriously indeed.

horse race normally takes place on the feast of the Assumption, though the Sienese are so enamoured of it that they run it at every opportunity. There is no set route through the city, but instead it is a madcap gallop to the Piazza del Duomo.

The build-up begins with impressive parades of flag-wavers, standard-bearers, trumpeters and drummers, all dressed in the most colourful costumes. Vast crowds fill the streets, passions run high and large sums of money are bet on the contestants. Frequent attempts (often successful) are made to bribe opposition jockeys to 'throw' the race and afterwards you may well see irate members of the crowd pursuing the losers. The jockeys are a tough breed, completely unscrupulous and more than happy to whip their opponents. The prize is a *pallium*, a piece of silk or damask cloth, padded with soft squirrel fur.

In recent times the most successful jockey has been Gostanzo Landucci, who has won the Palio on a number of occasions on his horse Dragon. He is quite a character, on one occasion being disqualified for jumping off at the finish and climbing the winning post. He is also a bad loser and complained bitterly when he felt he had beaten Lorenzo de' Medici's jockey but had to concede defeat (it takes a brave or foolish man to beat Lorenzo's candidate in anything). Landucci is a shrewd businessman – after selling his horse to the jockeys of Arezzo for forty florins, he proceeded to win it back in a race in that city.

PIENZA

Finally Sacchino's ass, which had been the winner often before, after throwing its rider, reached the winning-post first. The man who came in next still seated on his mount claimed that the first prize belonged to him rather to Sacchino, who had been thrown. The judges refused this plea on the grounds that the prizes were offered to asses, not men.

The little town of Pienza is largely the creation of Pius II following his election to the papacy in 1458 (he was born here as Aeneas Silvius Piccolomini in 1405). The architect, Bernardo Rossellino, laid out a series of palaces around a little piazza. Though a talented architect, Rossellino was also a Florentine and so needed to overcome the prejudice of the locals who accused him of cheating, incompetence and extravagance. The finest of his creations, the Palazzo Piccolomini, has three superimposed loggias looking onto a courtyard garden with Monte Amiata beyond. Pius II loved this mountain so much that he used to make his entourage go on picnics in the chestnut woods on its lower slopes, much to their stupefied amazement.

The highly ambitious Spanish Cardinal Rodrigo Borgia, anxious to promote himself with Pius, built himself a palace in the piazza, but rarely comes here as he is busy furthering his career in Rome, where he is a master of intrigue. He is also famed for his energetic love life and has at least seven illegitimate children.

Just a day's ride south-west of Siena lies the beautiful Cistercian abbey of San Galgano. There you will find a stone into which St Galgano thrust his sword back in the 12th century. Visitors from Britain may well see some parallels with their own legend of King Arthur, and some try to remove the sword in the hopes of being made king. Perhaps the ruthless English mercenary Sir John Hawkwood, a man used to having his own way, tried – certainly he went on to sack the abbey.

Before you leave Tuscany, make a final visit to the hilltop town of Montalcino, just off via Cassia near the southern boundary of the Sienese Republic. After enjoying a good lunch in the piazza, washed down by a bottle of the excellent local wine, sit back and take in the spectacular view. Such are the charms of this beautiful province, which has produced so many brilliant and talented individuals whose achievements have become the talk of Europe.

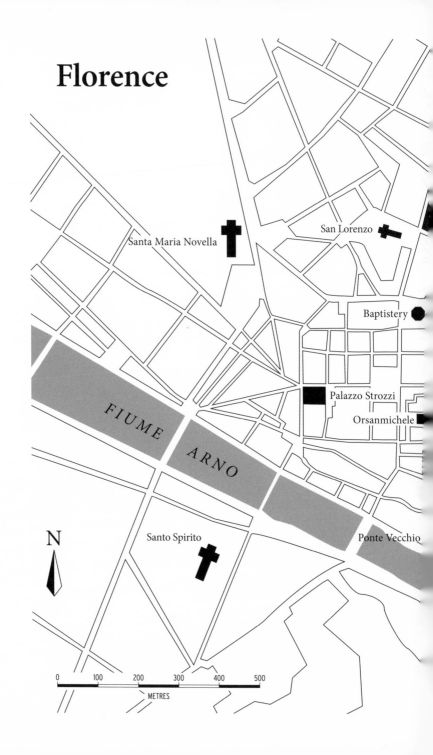

Convent of San Marco

zo Medici

Foundling Hospital

Duomo

Palazzo della Signoria

Santa Croce

UME   *ARNO*

AUTHOR'S NOTE

The setting for this guide is Florence in 1490. With the exception of notes on Michelangelo and Savonarola, a quotation from Vasari, and a few illustrations I have tried to make everything in the book consistent with that date. I would like to thank Eve Borsook and Ronald Lightbown for sharing their profound knowledge of the subject, and Francis Russell and Hugo Chapman for their suggestions for illustrations. I would also like to thank all at Thames & Hudson for their help. Lastly, I would like to dedicate the book to Jane who truly appreciates the miracle of Quattrocento Florence.

SOURCES OF QUOTATIONS

Numbers in brackets refer to the page in this book upon which the quotation appears.

H. Acton and E. Chaney, *Florence: A Traveller's Companion*, London, 1986 (8, 19, 56, 60, 62, 64); Dante Alighieri, *The Divine Comedy*, 3 vols (trans. J. D. Sinclair), New York, 1999 (9); *Art and Love in Renaissance Italy* (exh. cat.), New York, Metropolitan Museum, 2008 (14, 15); E. Borsook, *Companion Guide to Florence*, London, 1988 (42, 43); G. Brucker, *Renaissance Florence*, New York, 1969 (20, 27, 53, 78, 82, 109); K. Clark, *Leonardo da Vinci*, London, 1976 (49); C. Collier Frick, *Dressing Renaissance Florence*, Baltimore, 2002 (102); W. Connell, *Society and Individual in Renaissance Florence*, Berkeley, Calif., 2002 (57); R. Crum and J. Paoletti, *Renaissance Florence: A Social History*, New York, 2006 (24, 53, 83, 85, 109); J. Gage, *Life in Italy in the Times of the Medici*, London, 1968 (15, 19, 20, 44, 57, 67, 72, 86, 88, 136); F. Guicciardini, *The History of Florence* (trans. M. Domandi), New York, 1970 (45); J. R. Hale, *Florence and the Medici*, London, 1977 (47); C. Hibbert, *Florence: Biography of a City*, London, 1993 (70, 98, 102); J. Hook, *Lorenzo de' Medici*, London, 1984 (110, 124); J. Hook, *Siena: A City and its History*, London, 1979 (130, 131, 133); M. Levey, *Florence: A Portrait*, London, 1996 (6, 53); J. Lucas-Dubreton, *Daily Life in Florence* (trans. A. Lytton Sells), London, 1960 (100); N. Machiavelli, *The History of Florence* (ed. H. Morley), London, 1891; M. McCarthy, *Stones of Florence*, New York, 1959 (54); C. L. Mee, *Daily Life in the Renaissance*, New York, 1975 (17, 35, 77); J. M. Musacchio, *Art and Ritual of Childbirth in Renaissance Italy*, New Haven, 1999 (17); *Renaissance Siena: Art for a City* (exh. cat.), London, National Gallery, 2007–2008 (127); M. Rocke, *Forbidden Friendships: Homosexuality and Male Culture in Renaissance Florence*, New York, 1996 (33); A. Strozzi, *Selected Writings of Alessandra Strozzi* (trans. H. Gregory), Berkeley, 1997; M. J. Unger, *Magnifico: The Brilliant Life and Violent Times of Lorenzo de' Medici*, London, 2008 (45, 53, 75, 98, 109–10, 121); G. Vasari, *Lives of the Painters, Sculptors and Architects* (trans. J. Conaway Bondanella and P. Bondanella), Oxford, 1991 (56); *At Home in Renaissance Italy* (exh. cat.), London, Victoria & Albert Museum, 2006–2007 (11, 18); R. Weissman, *Ritual Brotherhood in Renaissance Florence*, New York, 1982 (87)

SOURCES OF ILLUSTRATIONS

Key: a=above, b=below, l=left, r=right

Biblioteca Medicea-Laurenziana, Florence 88
Biblioteca Riccardiana, Florence 81
British Museum, London 1, 73a, 79
From Bruschi 24
From *Canti carnascialeschi*, Florence, 15th century 104
From Jacobus de Cessolis, *Libro di giuocho di scacchi*, Florence, 1493 76
From Giorgio Chiarini, *Il libro de mercatantil*, Florence, 1490 2, 78
From *De Septem Vitiis*, late 14th century. British Museum, London 26

Duomo, Florence 50
Duomo, Lucca. Photo Alinari/Bridgeman Art Library, London 120b
Galleria degli Uffizi, Florence 8
Galleria degli Uffizi, Florence. Gabinetto Disegni e Stampe 48
From Christophoro Landini, *Formulario di lettere e di orationi volgare con lapro posta & ripost coposto*, Florence, 1492 32
Museo di Firenze com'era, Florence 6b
Medici Villa, Artimino. Photo Scala, Florence 6a, 11a, 22a , 44a, 53a, 72, 83a, 101a, 109, 115
From Lorenzo de' Medici, *Canzone per andare in maschera*, Florence, *c.* 1492 101b
Monastero di San Niccolo, Prato. Photo Bridgeman Art Library, London 120a
Museo Archeologico Nazionale, Florence 11b
Museo Nazionale del Bargello, Florence 56a, 56b, 59
Museo dell'Opera del Duomo, Florence 31, 54, 55, 73b
Museo dell'Opera Metropolitana, Siena 84
Museo di San Marco, Florence 67, 98
National Gallery, London 107
National Gallery, Washington, D.C. Samuel H. Kress Collection 7
Ospedale di Santa Maria della Scala, Siena 135
Palazzo Davanzati, Florence 18
Palazzo Pubblico, Siena 113, 132
Palazzo Vecchio, Florence 75
From A. Parmentier, *Album historique*, Paris, 1895 17, 23l, 23r, 25, 29, 44b, 53b, 65, 69r, 74b, 112, 123, 126, 127, 130
Royal Collection, Windsor Castle 49
Sala di Gualdrada, Palazzo Vecchio, Florence 28, 103
San Francesco, Arezzo 117
San Francesco, Prato. Photo Scala, Florence 119
Santa Croce, Florence 69l
Santa Maria Novella, Florence 63
From Girolamo Savonarola, *Compendio di revelatione*, Florence, 1495 99
Staatliche Graphische Sammlung, Munich 71
Victoria & Albert Museum, London 12, 47
Warburg Institute, University of London 83b, 105

COLOUR PLATE SECTIONS
Palazzo Pitti, Florence. Photo Alfredo Dagli Orti/The Art Archive, London I
Fitzwilliam Museum, Cambridge, lent from a private collection, London II
Palazzo Davanzati, Florence III
Santa Maria Novella, Florence IV
Galleria Nazionale delle Marche, Urbino V
National Gallery of Art, Washington, D.C. VI
Galleria degli Uffizi, Florence. Photo Erich Lessing/akg-images, London VII
Museo dell'Opera del Duomo, Florence VIII
British Museum, London IX
Palazzo Medici-Riccardi, Florence X
Museo di San Marco, Florence XI
Sala di Gualdrada, Palazzo Vecchio, Florence. Photo Scala, Florence XII
Museo Nazionale del Bargello, Florence. Photo Rabatti-Domingie/akg-images, London XIII
Palazzo Pubblico, Siena XIV
Museo di Firenze com'era, Florence XV
Palazzo Pubblico, Siena. Photo Scala, Florence XVI

INDEX

First published in the United Kingdom in 2010 by
Thames & Hudson Ltd, 181A High Holborn, London WC1V 7QX

thamesandhudson.com

British Library Cataloguing-in-Publication Data
A catalogue record for this book is available from the British Library

ISBN 978-0-500-25162-1

Printed and bound in China by Toppan Leefung Printing Limited